RANDOM THOUGHTS : *A Spiritual Journey*

BY JEAN ELIZABETH

Do you ever ask yourself why we are here? Every stage of our life brings us new challenges which must be dealt with. It is how we choose to deal with these challenges that define who we are, who we turn to when we are faced with great decisions which must be made.

These decisions are not easily and equitably resolved without looking within to find our inner strength. The author has faced challenges unlike most. She has had run ins with law enforcement, has been hosted by our governments lock up facilities, has faced health challenges which would defeat the least of us. As a result, she has great wisdom to share. That's the reason "Random Thoughts" came to be.

As Jean shares her history on these pages, she helps others by imparting wisdom beyond her years. A rape and kidnapping survivor, Jean Neary has lived through situations that would make the common person succumb, not want to wake up or take another step. Join her on her journey through life and accept this gift of insight.

Is your life all it can be? Do you wish to get more out of life? How do you find the inner strength to do the undoable, obtain the unobtainable, and survive the un-survivable? You will learn these skills among these pages. Let your journey begin.

Random Thoughts : A Spiritual Journey
Copyright © 2014 Jean Elizabeth
Edited by Patricia Logan
Cover Design & Formatting by JP Adkins

WARNING:

DEDICATION:

For the best grandma in the whole world because she never ever let me forget that to actually be an author one has to write a book. For my parents, because without them there would be no me! I love you so much. John, my love and gratitude for everything and all things, both big and small that you do to show your love and support.

Sasha, you have been the best Goddaughter I could ever imagine, for all the obvious reasons and for the reasons that will forever be secrets. Patti, you are the best BFF ever. Scout, you have always been one of the best gifts I have ever received. Bill, bet you are surprised to see yourself here and I am not even gonna tell you why.

Aunt Carol, you fostered a love for books and writing that has been my refuge. I have so much love and gratitude to my Instagram friends and writing group because I know if I had not gotten so much support for my writing I never would have committed to this book. A shout out to my adopted sister Maria, that phone call last year opened up a great chapter in my life. God, your grace and mercy saved me when I knew nothing would ever heal the wounds, inside and out, all the praise and glory to you.

IN THE BEGINNING

I wanted this book to be everything anyone would ever need to read for any occasion or reason. I could picture myself accepting one award after another for my brilliantly penned oratory about life and the hills and valleys that decorate it. People would stop me on the street asking for my autograph. Then, I woke up.

Hi! My name is Jean Elizabeth and I will guide you through the simple format and purpose of this book. I truly hope and pray you enjoy reading it as much as I loved writing it. I have been writing since I was in fourth grade and I never really had to struggle with it until I decided to write a book. I tried, tried, and could not even manage to come up with a rough outline. I decided that in the interest of my ongoing and future sanity I could put that story on a back burner and do a project I believe there is a need for: a positive, faith based, and informative guide for anyone interested in the temptations and pitfalls that surround us in the digital age we find ourselves in.

When I initially started to monitor my Goddaughter's phone and social media, I had no idea of the depth and scope of information traveling in real time between young adults. I was not watching her social media because she did anything wrong. I started watching because it gave me a glimpse into her world. I wanted to be a participant in her life choices and not just a spectator.

I read hundreds of books, talked to scores of people, used the internet so much that I thought I was going to break it, (lmao!), and consulted with doctors of all lifestyles about the gap in education where many of us never learned some of the simple things to make life less stressful and more peaceful. I am not a doctor, therapist, or member of the clergy and yet here I am, sharing my experience, strength, and hope, confident you will not regret taking the time to check out my journey. Interspersed throughout the book you will find poems, sayings, verses and some everyday information that are being used as tools to help you to focus on the good things, to focus your energy away from all the negative things, and to be the best human beings who you can possibly be.

There is an old saying that says "Don't judge a man until you have walked a mile in his shoes." This sentence is so important that I cannot overstate it. It is not my place to judge, it's my job to love and to do it to the very best of my ability. The only thing I judge is whether the relationships I enter into will be healthy for the people involved. I am an addict in recovery; there are people who have a personality that clashes with mine, and things become manipulative on both sides of the relationship. For my own peace of mind I choose not to pursue those friendships anymore; however, I still treat the individuals with love and respect.

The following statements are either true or false. This exercise is a good way to consider that people usually hide big parts of themselves and the person you think you know so well has only let you inside as much as they are comfortable. A healthy relationship is one in which secrets are shared as trust is validated and earned and it's a process that takes time and should be appreciated by everyone involved. However, if you meet someone who has a list like mine you might want to reconsider that invitation to dinner.

Some people tell you all their bad traits, bombard you with details of the horrible break-ups and relationship woes right away, and I think it's because they fear the end of the friendship if you ever really get to know the true person they are. We all have secrets and they tend to be secrets because were they to be revealed, it would cause a shift in your perception of the individual and a majority of the time it would be a negative shift. It is sad but many of us have self-esteem issues that go back as far as childhood. Some of the things we don't want to share are the secrets that cause guilt and shame and sadness. The secrets we try to bury are the hardest ones to get over personally and it feels like it would kill us to admit them to another human being. The point I want to make with this is simply that we only know about others what they want us to know. One of the most disrespectful and painful things to endure in a relationship occurs when secrets are revealed by someone who has no right to reveal them or tell your story.

If all you knew about me was the information below it would be understandable if you didn't want to get to know me better, in fact it might even be the intelligent choice. It would not be surprising to see our relationship falter because too much was revealed before you had a chance to begin building the foundation of a good relationship, developing trust and respect and both of those should be earned, not granted instantly . You don't find trust and respect at the bottom of the cereal box or in with your Cracker Jacks. The sum of my parts does indeed make the whole, but I am the first to admit that some of my parts are a bit shocking.

I have been in jail.

My relationship with my Creator and his son Jesus is the most important part of me.

I was a witness to death.

In my humble opinion, our criminal justice system needs a major overhaul. We spend crazy amounts of money keeping people healthy and comfortable in jail.

Our prisons are not deterrents. Many inmates live better in prison than on the streets. Again, this is my opinion.

I have had premarital sex, and I have been married and celibate.

4

Random Thoughts: A Spiritual Journey

I was the wheelman in an armed robbery and I didn't even know about it until years after the fact. The evening did involve mind-altering chemicals too.

I have not broken my wedding vows by being unfaithful.

Death is an acceptable outcome when survival is at stake.

I am a widow.

I was a bigamist. Accidently!

I have five aliases.

I was kidnapped. Twice!

I have made and lost one million dollars.

I have been homeless.

I have never sworn at or hit either one of my parents.

I did not learn how to clean a house correctly until my mid-thirties. I tried very hard but the concept was foreign to me.

I read quickly and voraciously.

I have stolen a Porsche.

I have seen evil and it kicked my butt.

The devil is not always ugly and menacing. A physically gorgeous man deceived me and he loved all the fear and evil he could generate.

I have served my country.

Random Thoughts: A Spiritual Journey

I don't regularly attend church but I love Joel Osteen and watch him every week.

I have tried most of the drugs available at the time I was partying.

I don't smoke. Anything

I became addicted to pain medicine after I fractured my back.

I am epileptic.

I have had a stroke.

I had a brain injury that scrambled my thoughts and movements for a decent amount of time. There is some organic brain damage.

My IQ is 136

I'm politically conservative (mostly).

I'm a big fan of the Ten Commandments.

When I die, I want to be remembered as a gentle warrior. I would love it if the thought of me causes someone I love to smile. Love is the best weapon.

On more than one occasion I have been forced to stare down the wrong side of a firearm.

Arriving home after a corporate Christmas Party there was a drunken man with an assault rifle on the roof of my apartment complex and he threatened the Vice President of the company I worked for who was kind enough to bring me home. The drunken dude was also my husband.

I was sued for sexual harassment when I was in my early twenties.

I tried rehab, but I wasn't ready. I got ready though.

Menopause turned me into a raving lunatic for a long time, it felt like years.

I had an eating disorder that lasted WAY to long.

There is nothing in life that matters more to me than the people I am blessed to know and love.

My Goddaughter is my sunshine.

I have two cats, they are brother and sister, and they were both rescue animals. I love them both to pieces.

I can't stand too much drama, and ANY drama is TOO MUCH drama.

I am a great friend.

I was a mud wrestler for a short time before I was old enough to be in the bar.

My alligator mouth overrides my hummingbird ass far more often than it should.

At the end of my party days and misspent youth I surrendered to the authorities knowing that I was looking at prison time because the last time I saw a judge he promised that consequence if I ended up back in court.

None of these is true!

All of these are true!

There is a measure of truth in each statement made.

There are two statements that are false and with some thought and common sense it's a piece of cake to figure it out.

I have chosen to write my book as almost a journal. Each page (and a page in this instance is the amount of space it takes to cover the topic of the day) has a quote or statement that is a doorway to knowledge of one kind or another. After the quote, the next section is an explanation or a personal story that enlarges on the topic. The third part is questions that allow you to decide if the topic is something you may need to work on to improve yourself or to help a loved one... Finally, the fourth part is either a prayer or an affirmation.

The format is simple and quite disorganized. The top of each "page" has a quote, poem, or thought and is followed by the body of the page discussing the particulars regarding the thought or quote. Thirdly, I ask a few questions about the topic so that you can do an internal check of your stance or belief in the hopes that if you are not satisfied with your answers you can take action and educate yourself fully. Each page ends with a short prayer or affirmation. It's a tool for meditation, growth or devotions and it is my prayer and heartfelt wish that our words bless your heart and offers you a new way to look at any given thought.

I have many wise and wonderful friends that have contributed pages and they are interspersed throughout the book like wonderful surprises. My faith is a huge part of my life and I share it openly but I believe there are huge differences between spirituality and religion and want to offer more than just my view. There are entries on exercise, diet, self-love, self-harm, sex, drugs, yoga and anything else I thought you might want to learn a bit about.

This book is not a textbook and I don't claim that all the information in this project is one hundred percent true. I will say that if there are lies, they are in order to protect someone and if there are little mistakes, I claim all of them myself. My prayer is that this book reaches out to young adults and their parents and helps bridge some of the gap between generations. The goal is to educate and foster better communication between all of us. Many of the issues in this book are not exactly happy shiny topics. There are times when generational or cultural gaps keep us from being understood and in my small way I am trying to improve that communication.

I am a survivor! I have had some amazeballs situations and circumstances occur that caused sweeping changes in my lifestyle, values, and spirituality. I am a Christian and much of the writing in my book comes from that place in my heart but it is not a book only for Believers. It took quite a while to go from a woman who had always believed in God because it's what I was taught as a child, to the woman I am today filled with the words of God and the joy that comes from being in a relationship with The Creator and his son, Jesus Christ.

The anecdotes I share while we travel through my book are about ninety-nine percent true. I had to change some names and places for some obvious reasons but embellishing the truth wasn't necessary, having seen and done some awkward things as well as some dangerous things. I pray that I learned from those encounters because the cost was so high I don't want to repeat it.

The list above gives you a small idea of my crazy life. I am not proud of my shenanigans, nor am I ashamed. It took the entire trauma to create the peace I now have and I would not change a minute. If you can learn from my mistakes, you are smarter than I am. it's my prayer that this book be a blessing in your life. It is worth it to me if it helps one person.

One of my primary goals with this book is to address the topics that are germane to the life you will embark on as an adult. I want to cover the high school years briefly, sex, drugs, music, God, religion, spirituality, diet, exercise, love, friendship, death, taxes and anything else I feel a burning desire to explore.

I'm obviously not in charge and all my lofty ideals would need a reality check if they ever got further than the fertile soil of my imagination but I hope and pray that this book makes you think, makes you smile and answers some questions you didn't even know you wanted the answers to. I wish you all years of true happiness and a life well lived.

Without further ado, welcome into my thoughts and dreams. May God bless you each day!

TRUST IS LIKE A MIRROR

Trust is like a mirror, you can repair it when it is broken, but you will always be aware of the crack in your reflection gazing back at you, a flaw that is like a weak link. In some instances, the trust is not merely cracked or broken but instead is shattered in thousands of pieces around you.

Trust is easily one of the cornerstones that help to build a solid foundation necessary to build relationships on and when that trust is betrayed so many things happen, one after the other, that it's very easy to be overwhelmed and paralyzed by all the feelings bombarding you from sunup to sundown.

Reestablishing trust is a lot to ask when you feel as though someone has run over your body, stopped, and in reverse run over you again. God is the only one that will never fail us and He can restore us from broken to whole.

I thought I was an open and honest person and when meeting new people would share or reveal shocking things as if they were normal occurrences. It was almost as if I was taunting my new friends, saying "see how crazy I am, are you sure you want to get to know me? I told you that once you got to know me you wouldn't want to be friends anymore. It happens all the time like this so go ahead and leave because we both know it's going to happen." It was a self-destructive way of trying to protect my heart.

When I meet new people now. I am an open and friendly person but I don't share all my secrets and skeletons within the first five minutes. In fact, I don't share some things at all unless by not sharing I'm causing a problem within the relationship. In addition, just because someone asks a question it does not obligate me to answer. A good example is the question "How many lovers have you had?" For me personally that's an awkward question and my response now would be "My past is my past and right now I don't feel as though I need to share that with you. I don't think it's appropriate or germane to the relationship to answer that question."

Trust should be earned and built in a relationship like walking up a flight of stairs. If you're on the bottom trying to get right to the top it's apparent that hurrying or skipping steps isn't healthy but I understand how tempting this is, however; if you walk step by step, allowing time and proximity to learn about each other you are forging a strong bond that time will only make stronger. If you hurry, you may fall.

Do you overshare or close up when meeting new people and is that perhaps giving others an inaccurate perception of you? Are you subconsciously pushing people away? Can you pray and concentrate on building a healthy relationship?

Lord, help me to remember that you are always there for us and let me listen well and take small steps with new people.

Random Thoughts: A Spiritual Journey
HITS & MISSES

If I could have anything, anything at all

it wouldn't be bling, or a shiny red ball,

I want to be loved, for real and truly,

Where I can giggle and feel all girly,

I want to tingle when I think of your kiss,

My score so far has been no hits and lots of misses.

THAT FIRST KISS IS VERY SPEICAL TO A LOT OF THE LADIES OUT THERE!

Our first kiss is a critical event,

If I adore you

But your kiss leaves me cold,

I'm honestly really sorry

But your love I cannot hold.

Kisses are a treasure

More precious to me than gold.

Forgive my forward words,

Allow me to be a bit bold,

If your kiss doesn't sizzle &

It's barely a fizzle

It's akin to striving for rain

Did he ask if he could kiss me? Some girls think that's gallant and cute if he asks permission and some think that's a precursor for being uncertain, not bold and confident! Was the kiss at the end of the date? Was it long, sloppy, wet, or dry? I didn't realize there were so many variables until the topic came up. I have always loved kissing and being affectionate and if a man kissed horribly and I really liked him I would do my very best to see if we could practice getting better at it together.

It isn't just the kiss that's important to many of us gals. Things like opening the door for us, making sure we are comfortable in the car, bringing a small token of affection as well as not going too overboard. I like a confident man but when it's too much it's arrogance and that can be a deal breaker. I cuss a lot but try to be sensitive and I appreciate other people that do the same thing.

One of my big turn-offs is a smoker. I am not a smoker and find it an unappealing habit. In the past, I dated men that smoked but now I know better. Why agree to a date with someone that smokes when I know how much I dislike it? If I really enjoy myself and like him, I try to convince myself it isn't a big deal but the reality eventually intrudes. I don't think it's fair to the smoker either. I would be unhappy and even though I

16

would be on my best behavior, that can't last forever. It seems dumb to date someone who does something I have no tolerance for. I don't really know any smokers who are alright with the smell, the cost and the public scrutiny and criticism they are confronted with while out on a date. Having said all that the big reason I won't date a smoker is that I know I will resent it and want him to change, and that's not fair to him.

Are you dating someone who already has a habit that is a deal breaker for you? Is that fair to either one of you? What other things are important to you when considering a future partner? Do you look for single people at activities that you enjoy such as bowling, dancing or going to a ball game?

We all deserve someone to spend our time with and there is the right person out there for me. I just need to continue being me while I wait for love to find me.

RELIGION IS LIKE ICE CREAM, THERE ARE TONS OF FLAVORS; LOVE SOME, HATE OTHERS — IT'S ALL STILL ICE CREAM.

I am passionate about my love for the Lord and the things I believe are right and wrong according to his Word. The simple way to explain it is biblical and makes it very easy to understand. God teaches us to love Him, love ourselves, and love others. If we do these three things to the best of our ability, we find that the Ten Commandments are followed as a result.

As I was growing up, I decided nobody could tell me how to feel or believe about anything. I could make up my own mind after exploring and experiencing things in life. I started out Catholic and to this day, there are many things about the Catholic faith that I think are true and beautiful. I love the mass in Latin. The church is all about the family and the community and that too is a good thing. I love that Catholics see God as a force to be respected. They demand respect for God and I have to agree. No blue jeans and T-shirts when I attended mass.

I took a class in school on ancient religions in the western civilizations and developed more hypotheses and ideas. I liked Buddhism, pieces, and parts of many religions and belief systems. I have a close friend that is a psychic (Hi Scout!) and he helped me shape some of my thoughts.

The bottom line is that after exhaustive research and prayer I think that there is only one God, and he is quite confident in himself. Most religions are actually quite similar and I try not to argue dogma unless someone is on the same search I was on and just wants to know what I think. Religion is a manufactured thing that accomplishes some key tasks. A moral outline helps society function. It tries, in some cases, to control the population and generate income to achieve its objectives. There is some emotional and mental manipulation to achieve objectives in behavior modification.

My prayers and well wishes are with you if this is a place you find yourself and I am confident you will solve the questions for yourself and make your decision.

Are you questioning your beliefs? Are your questions making you feel more solid or shakier?

Do you feel like now is a good time to develop your spiritual identity?

Lord, help us as we go through each day to recognize the truth, hear your voice, and love in the things we see and do.

JUST BECAUSE YOU DON'T TAKE AN INTEREST IN POLITICS DOESN'T MEAN POLITICS WON'T TAKE AN INTEREST IN YOU.

There is no perfect political party nor is there a perfect candidate. One of the crucial things to keep in mind is the fact that we live in the United States and we have the best people, the most beautiful land, and rights and responsibilities as citizens. One of those responsibilities is voting. I enjoy debating politics but when I'm going neck to neck with someone, whose passion is explosive and they believe their view is gospel, I quietly ask if they vote.

If you don't participate in the political process in any way perhaps your loudly offered opinion and criticism should be tempered or educated. We have a responsibility as Americans to uphold the constitution and the Bill of Rights and part of that task is voting. We are so blessed to have the opportunities and freedoms that we have in this country. Participation in the political process directly affects all of our lives and if you have not voted before I encourage you to dip your toe in the pond of politics. Local politics directly affect you and in some big ways. State and federal politics shape the way we live as well.

Lastly, in order to make the most informed decision about whom to cast your ballot for, listen to both sides of the issue. Commercials and sound bites are designed to grab you and make you feel strongly, either for or against the issue or candidate, and I would encourage getting online and reading some of the mainstream media as well as listening to at least one debate.

I am a conservative about most things political and I am embarrassed to say I didn't have even the slightest scintilla of interest about all things political until I met President Clinton. For some reason his magnetic personality, passion, and innate intelligence, quickened the desire to know more about the leaders of our country and I am grateful that we have had some compelling people and issues to nurture my thirst for knowledge in this arena. It is an honor and a privilege to be in the United States of America and it's our responsibility to vote and support our elected officials.

Do you think you pay enough attention to the politics in the place you live? Could you do more to educate yourself and by voting include yourself in the process?

Lord, Protect and guide the leaders of our country and thank you for the freedoms we enjoy by living in the best place on the planet. We know that no weapon formed against us will prosper.

IT'S LATE TONIGHT

And I'm ready to unwind, to relax and let go, to lie down and shed the rigid control, my waking hours are flanked by hush little one let not your heart be troubled I am a leaf on a the wind, watch me soar.

It took me years to find a way to ramp down after a day of fighting in the trenches. I was born in what I believe to be a simpler time. We lived in a medium size town but I knew every neighbor on our street as well as the two streets next to us. To make extra money I raked leaves in the fall, shoveled snow in the winter, and washed cars in the spring and summer. My parents had me take care of a widow and a disabled person for free and I never once questioned why. It was the way folks were.

Twenty years later, I lived in a medium size town and did not even know the neighbors on either side of me… and I lived in an apartment! The pace of life seemed so accelerated that I felt out of breath regularly, and it was difficult to make time for random acts of kindness when it seemed we were all treading water just to keep from drowning.

Today I make the time to do the things that allow me to breathe easier. I pray frequently and it's not a formal, kneel down and bow my head type of thing. It's more like for everything I do I check with the Lord before, during and after whatever task I am involved in. The bible teaches us how to pray in the book of Matthew and I take the time for that form of communion regularly as well. If you could see and hear me most of the time, it would sound like I am talking to a best friend, teacher, and parent all rolled into one.

I focus on the things I can do to make the people around me feel noticed and valued. An example of this type of love is complimenting strangers on their appearance or something they did that was thoughtful or even just meeting a person's eyes and smiling a genuine greeting. When I'm in the line at the store I pay attention and do little things like help people unload their cart or let someone go in front of me with a few items.

If you alter your perceptions and behavior to reflect this willing kindness I am sure you will notice the smile that comes more often, the feeling of contentment with a job well done, or just the subtle understanding that it is not ALL ABOUT YOU.

A short personal note: yes, I love Firefly and Serenity and that's where the last line in the poem comes from! The line above that comes from Sean Hannity.

Do you wear blinders as you go through the day? Are you in such a rush that you don't practice willing kindness? Do you find yourself in a pensive mood anytime you have to interact with people you don't know?

Lord, help me to be an example of you to those I meet. Make me an instrument of your peace and let me plant seeds of kindness and love in all of my actions.

WHEN CHOOSING FRIENDS AND PEOPLE TO HANG OUT WITH, TRY TO KEEP IN MIND THAT WATER SEEKS ITS OWN LEVEL!

The important thing to pay attention to when choosing friends, companions and even co-workers is that like attracts like and lies attract even worse lies. I was a bit of a contradiction as a teen because academics were fairly easy for me and getting good grades was expected and I produced. As I began taking college classes while in high school I got distracted by all the well intentioned kids who thought I would be less stressed if I smoked pot. They were right!

By my junior year of high school I had a solid and dependable GPA, I had a job and some very good friends that I spent time with on the weekends and after school, and I partied whenever I had the chance. It was a magical time to me. My best friend lived next door and we were inseparable for a couple of years. I still think about her and say a prayer for her.

It didn't take long for me to end up sitting across the desk from our dean and he was shaking his head as if I just confused him even more than usual and he would appreciate it if I would settle down and get my head straight. He explained that I was in the top ten percent of our class, was always polite, respectful to my teachers, and considering all those facts, why was I also one the people selling pills, and pot on campus?

I didn't have a glib answer for that and I also noticed there were no police hanging out in the halls. This was a very welcome realization because if I was going to be in legal trouble they would already be involved by joining our little meeting. I wasn't sure exactly what the plan was but I figured honesty was a good foundation to build on. I wasn't going to volunteer details but I knew and trusted him and was positive that he would be careful about anything I did reveal. After another five minutes of conversation, he shook his head one last time and asked me to get myself sorted. Surprisingly, I did listen and stop the drugs, both the buying and the selling.

People didn't intentionally try to bring you down to their level but it happens anyway. If you used to drink and get high it was fun to get a group together and have a party in the desert. Those were good times. When I quit all that, I found that my friends were sloppy when they were drunk, made almost no sense when they were high on speed or pot, and they kept trying to talk me into partaking of the party supplies. Then it just seemed like we didn't have much in common anymore and our orbits changed so that we didn't see each other much.

Have you made a positive lifestyle change recently? Are your peers supportive or trying to talk you back into the fold? Are you noticing that things aren't as comfortable when you are the only one abstaining? Are you now seeing who your true friends are?

Lord, thank you for the positive changes in my life. Please bring likeminded people into my life to help support my good changes. Help me also to see the friends of mine that may also want to change for the better.

"WHATEVER" HAS BECOME A FOUR LETTER WORD!

I am so exhausted by people who upon disagreement with me, instead of calmly and respectfully talking about it, they utter the word WHATEVER! It's not just the word that grinds my gears, it's the gestures and tone and the body language that accompanies the proclamation.

I have talked to hundreds of people and this is one of the few things that is universally agreed upon. I feel that when I am attempting a conversation that may be a mite controversial the last thing I want to hear from the listener is "whatever". It implies complete disgust and disdain and the thought that I am too stupid to understand a different point of view, so instead of arguing, the listener bails on the whole deal. This is a passive-aggressive tactic, which causes me to envision some of the lesser forms of torture as a tool to effect better communication.

I am cognizant that I am unreasonable on this issue. I think "whatever" is a four-letter word and you might as well say "fuck you" if you're going to metaphorically deliver it. Inevitably, the people using this form of insult refuse to admit that there is any disrespect intended or implied and they smile with that insincere grin that never reaches the eyes. I am sure there are folks out there that don't believe that saying whatever is anything more than a way to communicate disinterest, but I think the majority are completely aware of how that response is perceived.

I had a boyfriend that used to say that every time a conversation got in the slightest bit controversial. I magnanimously admit that I am a tad bit rabid about this point. My history with the boyfriend and the response both sucked and as a result I try to avoid anything that causes this trigger to slap me in the face. I am not always successful but there has been some infinitesimal improvement in the last couple of years. I no longer scream, pull my hair out or throw things when the frustration hits the red zone.

We all have words, phrases, and behaviors that trigger an overreaction due to our history. Being aware of the issue is a big step and for the most part, once we realize it's a hot button we can take a tiny step backward emotionally and react like calm human beings.

Do you know what your triggers are? Have you resolved the pain that caused those triggers to develop in the first place? Have you written out the incident or person that caused your reaction to be so negative? Are you careful not to turn around and use your triggers on other people?

Lord, help me to forgive the person that caused these hurts and let me forgive me for losing control when my buttons are pushed. Grant me the serenity to know if this is one of the things I can change or one of the things I just have to accept. Thank you for soothing my spirit when I feel so attacked.

RESCUING AN ANIMAL COULD SAVE YOU!

My rescue cat Goober just spent ten minutes smacking my face with his tail with an attitude. I was subjected to this display of feline temper because he sat down by a new package of kitty treats and they didn't magically open and allow him to eat his fill before they magically closed up and jumped back into the cabinet. His answer was to use his claws and drag the treats out into the middle of the floor so he could expend maximum energy using claws, teeth, and physics to put a hole into the treats, at which point he declared victory and purred so loud and smiled so big I started to laugh and couldn't stop.

Throughout my life, I have had times where we had pets and times where they were not allowed. I am a pet person. I like the playing and affection and usually all I have to provide is food and water and it makes me the best mom ever in the history of the world.

I have had hamsters, guinea pigs, cats, dogs, a goat, rats, mice, and a snake. All pets help teach us responsibility for another being. If you neglect your pet enough it will become feral and die. Perhaps because I did not have children, I got very close to my pets.

Currently I have two rescue cats that are litter-mates. My boy is the Goober and his sister is the Squeakers. They are both six years old and spoiled rotten. The interesting thing about my babies is that they are from a feral litter and my vet, whom I dearly love, encouraged me to take both of the kids. They were the last two in the litter and the mom was gone so we got two new kitties.

They are polar opposites. Goober is twenty-four pounds of huge! He is full of love and has never had a bad day except after the night he fell off the cat perch while sleeping and hurt his back a little bit. He follows me from room to room and when he wants affection, he will be relentless until he gets it and is satisfied with the quality of the offering.

Squeakers is a very unique young kitty. She was born of a feral litter, is still quite skittish,

and she has a spinal injury that affects the way she holds herself as well as her interaction with others, feline as well as human. She is six years old and you cannot pick her up or catch her unless she wants you too. She only comes out from under the bed when the house is quiet or there is golf on TV.

We have been sensitive and gentle with her and do not rush her healing. It took years before I could pet her as she streaked by. Five years later, we have a great routine. She has her own pillow on the bed and she likes to observe from there. She loves being brushed as well as receiving treats. I can kiss her on the top if her head now but it took years before she trusted that I wouldn't throw her in a cage and feed her to the lions. I did not believe I had the patience and sensitivity to nurse her out of her personal hell and into the bosom of our family but thankfully I was wrong.

The point I'm making is that life has damaged all of us, some more than others, but healing is possible. I can't envision another family adopting my little scared cat. Six years and she still does not want to be cornered or picked up by anyone. She does come up to us for treats, brushes and love. She will kiss us on the forehead if we quietly and patiently wait for her to get up the courage to act. She plays with her brother now and I can't imagine not having her.

Is there someone in your life that needs a little extra TLC? Can you show some extra sensitivity with someone that is struggling to heal? Are you taking onto yourself someone else's pain?

Lord, help me to be sensitive to all your creatures, both big and small. Let me feel the correct way to share your love with the broken people I meet. Thank you for caring for each one of us, just as you care for the birds in the trees.

ARE YOU A GLASS HALF-FULL OR A GLASS HALF-EMPTY TYPE OF PERSON?

There are optimists, pessimists, and people that fall somewhere in between. I have experienced such horror and tragedy that you would expect me to be full of fear and foreboding about the future but the opposite is true. I am joyful and hopeful, I choose to focus on the good and beautiful in each day, and I believe that attitude helps ensure a positive outcome.

When I was fifteen, a teenage prostitution ring targeted me. That was the first scary thing I had to endure. I went to my parents and we decided that the best way to deal with the problem would be for me to leave until things were resolved. I spent three months almost three-thousand miles away from my parents and siblings. I believe that this experience helped shape the strength I have needed to draw on so many times throughout my journey.

On my seventeenth birthday, I was abducted at gunpoint and knew I was gonna die. I believe God intervened and allowed me the opportunity to disable one of my attackers and run for freedom. I knew the men responsible and I had to search my heart trying to understand how something so terrifying happened to me. I finally stopped saying "why me?" and started saying "why not me?" This incident caused my family to pull up stakes and move to another state.

When I was eighteen I was playing around with a man I had met recently; we were wrestling, he accidently landed on me, and I fractured my spine. I was in a corset and various braces for quite some time and the pain was constant. That happened two weeks before I was supposed to report for basic training in the Marine Corps. I am fiercely patriotic and was crushed to have to give up my dream.

Life went on and I had the option of breaking under the weight of the sorrow or becoming stronger. What doesn't kill us does indeed make us stronger. Every single person I know has had to deal with tragedy and hardship. It's just a part of life and the truth is that if we didn't have the terrible times, the good times wouldn't be as sweet. Balance is one of the keys to a happy life. It does no good to spend time in the past asking "why me?" because the truth of the matter is "why not me!"

One of the best things I do for myself and the people I love is that I choose to focus on the positive aspects of every single situation. When your heart and spirit is constantly searching and being grateful for even the smallest of positive things, a shift occurs that really makes a difference. It's difficult to quantify but it's almost like the air you breathe gets sweeter. It's a challenge to alter your focus in that direction and it doesn't come overnight but I know that my heart is lighter than it has ever been and I am so very grateful.

In my relationships with others, this shift in focus was like adding fertilizer to the soil in my garden. All of my friends are precious to me and I noticed the difference in myself as well as in my loved ones when I focused on sharing good thoughts. Something as simple as complimenting an outfit or as complex as acknowledging a lifestyle change that is painful, everyone responded in a good way. I didn't feel a need to share the change inside me but I have had a couple of my friends ask me what I'm doing different. I tell them I'm praising the Lord in all things and focusing on feeding the angel on my shoulder instead of the Devil on the other shoulder.

Are you a blessing to your friends and family? Do you take the time to focus on and comment about the little things in a positive way? Have you noticed an increase in your happiness level and the happiness of the people around you?

Lord, help me to share your love and kindness with all those I meet and put a guard over my mouth that I may not sin against you. Help me to see your loving hand in all my affairs and thank you for the heart and mind of Christ.

> *Take a stroll down to Lucifer's Lair*
>
> *You and he would make quite a fine pair*
>
> *He's father of lies, king of them all*
>
> *See what hell you can buy*
>
> *You can't take the big fall*
>
> *Get Drunk, Get Laid, Put on a Grin*
>
> *The door to hell is open*
>
> *He say's, "Come on in!"*

As Believers, we are constantly sensitive to the fight between good and evil. It is something we are aware of inside ourselves, our home, our family, our city, our state, and globally. For me, it goes back to intake and focus. What am I feeding my mind and spirit and what is taking most of my focus?

For example, I read a lot. It's one of my favorite things to do and my interests are quite varied. When I'm reading secular fiction and have been ingesting mysteries or murder, death, kill books, it doesn't surprise me if I have bad dreams or if my mood gets a little dark. I don't think there is anything wrong with secular fiction and some of the Christian fiction that's available is also dark in content but I need to remember to keep it balanced.

When I first embraced a relationship with God, I spent a fair amount of time praying and meditating on what God's plan for my life would be. I didn't feel any pressure in one direction or the other but I also felt a little like a boat with no rudder. I wasn't hearing the still small voice of God. I knew I was making good decisions but that was mostly because I was following the laws of the land and striving to follow the laws of God.

One night I was ruminating on this situation and I heard a voice just like it was in the next room. It said "how are you supposed to recognize my voice if you don't know my Word."

I have spent copious amounts of time in the bible throughout my life but I had forgotten that the bible is spiritual food. Taking just fifteen minutes in the morning to do my devotions made a significant difference in the quality of my days. I just open it up to wherever it falls and go from there.

Are you paying attention to what your mind, body, and spirit are eating? Is your diet as balanced as you can make it? Are you keeping in mind the axiom GIGO (garbage in/garbage out)?

Lord, help me keep balance in my days and remember to feed my mind and spirit as well as my body.

BUT, WE WERE SOUL MATES AND IN LOVE, WHAT CHANGED?

I thought we were perfect for each other and then after we got married everything changed. Why do we still have over fifty percent of the people getting married getting divorced within seven years? The average amount of time new relationships are in the honeymoon phase tops out at eighteen months. We all know about the wonder of getting to know the perfect person that will seamlessly fit into our lives and there will never be anything but sunshine and laughter forevermore. Every eccentricity and little habit is adorable and both people are on their best behavior. I have learned that if I continue to treat my man like we just got together and I am grateful for everything, then he is also still very happy and thoughtful. I have heard him tell several people that one of the things that is important to him is the fact that I do not take him for granted and I am still grateful for even the "small" things.

When I was searching for a life partner, I would find someone attractive and proceed from there. I may go on a few dates and spend some time together and as long as things were good and that attraction was still humming, I would let sex catapult into the fledgling relationship. There is nothing evil and wrong with sex in a personal relationship but it has some consequences when it happens early in the mix. The process of building a strong friendship allows for disagreement and discovery of our differing opinions and actions.

When sex is a part of the mix, the tendency is to be quiet and have sex to feel good instead of the protracted conversations involved in truly getting to know someone. It's not a conscious decision, it's simply that the dynamic changes. The thing to consider is that sex is awesome, fun and beautiful, and the gateway to having children, and as all these things, it is hugely important in the first decade of marriage.

All I'm really trying to say is that sex is huge and important and maybe shouldn't be introduced into a relationship before you have had a dozen dates. I used sex as a cure-all for whatever ailed me and now thirty years later, it is the only regret I truly have. Specifically, I regret that I treated sex like a fun way to spend time, a sport that's also a fun way to spend time, a complicated version of a handshake, and most importantly, I didn't see it as a way to share the totality of who I am with someone I cared for in the hopes of enriching an already strong friendship.

Do you treat sex and your body with disrespect? Are you using sex as a bandage or to avoid intimacy? Do you treasure and cherish your body as well as your partners?

Father God, let us see the beauty of relationships when founded on strong spiritual principles. Let love and respect always be ours to guard and cherish when we share them with others in intimacy.

SHARING WITH A LITTLE HELP FROM MY FRIENDS!

There will be samples of many of my friends writing. Most of us are on Instagram and next to the name of the author is their Instagram profile. Many of us write free verse, poetry, haiku, or whatever we see inside that begs for a voice on the outside.. There are constantly contests that force us to stretch our reach and grasp for more. I have been writing since I was nine years old and only with the support of these people could I finally put pen to paper and get my book written. My best friend let me write a poem that she published in one of her early books. If you ever want to see my poetry, or just say hi, my Instagram name is jeanElizab3th. Welcome to the jungle.

My only regret with this book is that I can't include the gorgeous and amazeballs art that is all over the place on Instagram.

***

Random Thoughts: A Spiritual Journey

Let me use the word of unrequited fame.

Allow me to use the word which sounds all too cliché.

Please let me give you a title which you do deserve

Let me call you beautiful, and pardon my nerve.

But don't give me arguments about your looks,

For I will simply give you the simile of covers and books.

Forget about the appearances darling, I don't care about your hair.

I want to look inside of you, there are troves of treasure there.

For beautiful in looks? Sure, that's nice to be

But your fierce little soul is what's beautiful to me.

I can see it in the pages which you so carefully write

I see it in the way your little lips sweetly whisper "goodnight."

-Author: Lilian (Museofseventeen)

There are some who move rocks with facts but lack passion, while there are others who move mountains with great passion but lack facts, & then there are the select few who change the world by possessing both.

-Author: Michael T. Coe,(IG: audio_bomb)

***

I crack a smile

Convinced this is worthwhile

Breathtaking memories surround my mind

Sincerity and clarity

I need to clarify

Say what's in my heart

Must be out of my mind not to try this

Sweet melody fills me with bliss

So far away but so worth the wait

My heart and mind cannot debate

This feeling is true and pure

I cannot abstain

All my feelings convene

Nothing will intervene

How beautiful this can be.

-Author: Maria Quan (Official_MQ)

A FEW THINGS I HAVE LEARNED...

When you give, do so quietly and in abundance.

When you take, do so carefully and according to your need.

When you seek help, ask knowing that your needs will be met.

When you are grateful, express your thanks honestly and with passion.

When you are hungry, eat what you need trying not to waste so that others also can be fed.

When you are tired, sleep the sleep of innocents knowing you do your best every day.

The older I get the simpler life seems to me. When I was twenty-one I was an adult and made my own choices and decisions. I didn't consider anything global in nature because I thought my one voice wouldn't sway or change any big global issue.

When I was thirty my focus was on my home and my family. We were trying to have a baby and had bought our first home. I had a job that I liked and they became a second family of sorts. I cared about the happiness of the people around me and discovered that I got great joy when I was able to help another human being do something that was difficult for one but simple with two.

When I was forty my worldview had expanded and changed and I now cared about everyone in one manner or another. I began doing things to help our veterans because that is where my heart resides. I started recycling because it was easy and made sense. I could see that all the disposable trash was going to one day be a big deal if things didn't change in a big way. I vote in every election because these are the people charged with making some tough decisions and I wanted to know the people making decisions that would affect me. I also gave some time and energy to helping people hook up with the perfect pet. I worked with rescue animals because I believe that they know we save their lives and they love us for it.

I turn fifty soon, my life is rich with content, and I am wealthy in all the things that matter to me. I have a goddaughter that is the biggest blessing I have ever received. My best friend shares her daughter with me selflessly and completely and I adore both of them for letting me love them and having their love in return. I am a member of their family and they are mine. I work with teens in crisis and the way the world is today, lots of kids can use a little help along the way and I am honored to be there. It really was a simpler time when I was growing up but I had the same issues to get through that today's teens struggle with. Body image and self-esteem issues are paramount and eating disorders are common. Family conflict, drugs, and alcohol have always been a problem.

Do you think about the ramifications before you act? Is your viewpoint myopic or global or somewhere in between? Are you a functioning member of your family? Do you give as you can and take as you need? Do you vote and pay attention to politics, either locally or on a bigger scale? Do you help others less fortunate that you?

Lord, help me today to see the people around me as you see them. If someone needs a helping hand or a hug let me be there to give it. Make me an instrument of your peace. Let my actions show my love and my heart and let my words reflect that same truth.

CONTROLLING ADDICTION IS LIKE HERDING CATS. JUST BECAUSE EVERY SO OFTEN THEY GO WHERE YOU WANT THEM TO IT DOES NOT MEAN YOU HAVE ANY CONTROL OVER THEM AT ALL.

I have been dealing with addiction as long as I can remember. My parents are recovering alcoholics and most of my family has dabbled in addiction in one form or another. Thankfully, we are all in recovery and I love my family now with a healthy but fierce love that continues to grow as time goes by.

I attended my first twelve-step meeting in December of 1981 and it was immediately a warm and welcome place to be. My mom always says you can meet the best and the worst people in the world at a meeting. I have seen the transformation when the program begins to work; it's magic in the life of someone who no longer thinks they have any worth. Their entire life has come crashing down around them and for a long time they simply focus on not drinking or using in that moment, that hour and that day. They then go on to become the person they were born to be. I have met the most loving and generous people in my life in those meetings and while I don't celebrate being an addict I certainly celebrate the lifesaving event of walking through the doors at my first meeting.

I have met people that are trying to control their addiction. They have complex formulas and rules that they believe if they can keep their use of whatever substance they are fond of within their rules then they are not an addict. It is recreational or social use. My favorite example of this is cocaine. First of all it's not legal and if you are caught buying, selling or using it your life will change drastically, and not for the better. Second, the nature of this particular drug is all about doing more. I got to the point with my own use of cocaine that when I bought it on Friday I was immediately planning how to get more when I would run out. I never made a good decision under the influence. The least harmful thing I did was play a lot of cards with people who were just as high as I was.

Then I moved on to speed. That was a train wreck because it did give me more energy and I did become more productive. It had the added bonus of causing me to lose so much weight that I was ninety-four pounds when I finally was shot of that mess. I knew what drugs to use if you want to make methamphetamines and I still ingested it every single day. I was in an untenable situation personally at that time but my addict thinking told me that it was manageable as long as I had dope. I should have walked out without ever trying it. The first time I did crank, I painted our house in one weekend and everyone was so happy about my amazing energy. When I quit, I slept for three days and was weak as a kitten but I didn't touch it again. Praise the Lord!

Are you in denial about your addiction? Have you had a bad time but still have things to lose? Has your use caused you to have problems in any area of your life? Are you self-medicating to hide something else? Have you seen a doctor to see if you have a chemical imbalance? (Most of us do!)

Lord, put the right person in the path of our addiction. Let us hear about your healing love and peace. Help to heal our bodies, minds, and spirits as we walk into recovery. Let us give back to those that so desperately need it.

EVERYBODY SUFFERS TRAGEDY! IF THERE WAS NO PAIN, HOW WOULD WE RECOGNIZE JOY?

At two pm in a busy town I was grabbed off a busy street, and nobody saw a thing. Forty-five days later, I stumbled into a post office in a town I had never heard of and called for help. It was two am, I had no money, no clothes except what were on my back, and I was afraid of just about everything.

The very first thing that my abductor said to me was "Hi, I'm Tony and I have been hired to kill you. You have three days to convince me you are not guilty of the charges your husband has brought against you. I want you to know you will not be tortured (that ended up not being the truth, however, he never tried to hurt me) and I will not drag out your death for hours or days of suffering. They say that you have betrayed your family (not my blood family) and attempted to put them in prison. I am taking you somewhere safe so we can sit down and talk and I'm telling you now that you don't want to attempt to escape. That would force me to kill you immediately. We are going to be in a kind of remote place and we can stop by the store first to get you anything you need for a couple of days."

Therefore, we stopped at the store and picked up the stuff so I could make him all his favorite Italian foods from scratch. I was determined to live and I was stunned and shock was beginning to set in but I heard what he said and understood that he wasn't bluffing or even trying to frighten me. He was just telling me how things were going to happen. I knew there was a fair amount of people responsible for this act and I would have to deal with a mountain of lies at the same time as I was feeling so much rage I couldn't stop shaking.

My husband and I had a beautiful home and a successful business that we both worked very hard to create and it was something we loved and were proud of. Things had declined personally between us over the last year and I finally knew if I didn't leave I was going to die. I'm not being over dramatic either. He had informed me of his displeasure and some of his friends had gone so far as to hold me with a gun to my head on more than one occasion.

I walked out on him carrying two gym bags with what I wanted to keep from all the things we owned. It would have set me up for three or four years if I lived very frugally. The police apprehended me before I made it out of the driveway. The next eight hours were so painful that I have blocked big parts of them completely.

I eventually ended up at the only people's house that I knew from earlier days and was there for about ten days before they found me. This started my abduction and they would move me from one place to another, passing me off to different groups of people who wanted various things from me. I am positive there are people in the world that have suffered far more than I did during my tenure with some of the craziest people I have ever met. Like everything else in life, it was not all horrible. There were a couple of people that didn't like what was happening to me and they did stuff like bring me food or a book to read and I thank God for them.

What I'm getting at is that we all have something horribly painful we have had to overcome in order to find peace and some measure of personal happiness. I am blessed that my ordeal actually allowed me to have the knowledge to help other victims of violent crime. I watched one such individual go from being afraid of people and hating to be touched to holding my hands while he cried for joy that he was not a delusional schizophrenic; he was a victim of an obscene crime against himself.

Have you identified the tragedies in your life? Have you allowed time to help heal your scars into stars? Have you been able to gain inner strength from the bad times? Do you still live in the past where things are still so painful? Have you found someone you trust to talk to about your ordeal?

Joy does indeed come in the morning. God promises us beauty for ashes, the oil of joy for mourning, and the garment of praise for the spirit of heaviness. I am a seed of righteousness, a planting of the Lord that he might be glorified. (Book of Isaiah).

TO SURRENDER IS NOT ALWAYS TO LOSE, SOMETIMES IT'S MOVING OVER TO THE WINNING SIDE!

When I escaped my captors, I ran quickly and found a place to disappear. Within twenty days, I had moved, changed my name and appearance, and gotten a job. I had a huge amount of incentive to make a clean break from my past and I followed some simple but important rules. A feeling of unexplained dread always shadowed me and it was exhausting. It felt as though I was swimming through a marsh of cotton candy. Everything was scary in a wispy, sticky, and icky way.

I did not work in the field I did previously. It sucked because I had years of school and years of experience in my field but it's a specialized arena and everybody either knew or had heard of everyone else. To make matters even more difficult I was a specialist in a very small part of a very small field.

I also happened to be on formal probation. I was on probation in the first place because I was an idiot and was being stupid with almost an ounce of crank on me at the time. I believe God ordained everything that happened because of that arrest because it ended up saving me instead of making a hard situation even worse. My probation officer told me the truth from the very first time I saw him.

He calmly sat across from me and said, "Let me tell you why you are on probation, why I am your probation officer who only handles felonies that are drug related, and where we believe we can infiltrate the organization the felon is affiliated with. I was initially confused about why your file even crossed my desk but after reading the entire file twice, I think I get it. You were apprehended with a large amount of methamphetamines and cash and a fair amount of diamonds and other precious stones. This caused the arresting officer to make some incorrect (I believe they were wrong) assumptions about who you are. You have never been arrested before and that actually says quite a bit about you. In addition, you have only been married for a short time and I don't even know if you are aware of who you husband is and who he belongs to. The other thing I couldn't figure out is why your charges were dropped to misdemeanors. You had the drugs bundled for sale and had $500 in cash. Can you explain that to me?"

"Sure I can tell you what happened, I had the cash, the dope, $7,000 in opals and $20,000 in diamonds and when I was contacted to come pick up my property they released everything to me. I got my cash, my jewels, and my dope all given back in my backpack. Initially I was afraid it was a set-up so we disposed of the dope within three minutes and drove the speed limit all the way home. And, just so you know, my husband was armed and I had dope on me that I shoved in between the seat cushions in the cruiser I was in. I was armed in the car but did not take it inside with me and so was not arrested with it. I wouldn't have been caught with the dope except one of the store clerks recognized my paraphernalia and called out to the cop as he was writing me a ticket. She told me I would thank her someday. She's wrong about that." I explained quietly but with determination.

Bob, that was his name, laughed for at least two minutes! Good to know he had a good sense of humor. I was going to need that before we were all done.

I was nervous about the whole probation thing because the group my husband was a part of did not like the situation at all and every time I got home from my appointments, someone was waiting at the house to inform me of the things discussed and what I was to say next time. Eventually they would encourage me to pretend to flip on the group and they fed me whatever information they wanted shared.

I was allowed to continue using drugs as long as they thought I was being cooperative but as soon as I refused a request, I was drug tested and arrested to serve the sentence that was suspended initially. I was naively surprised that I never got drug tested during my monthly reporting until I stopped playing their game. I served about six weeks because I started out on house arrest but like an idiot, I failed the drug test. House arrest and jail are like apples and rifles, there is no comparison.

During my incarceration, I rededicated my life to God and attended church and Bible study while I was there. My life outside was so fraught with tension and danger that I actually enjoyed jail. I had never spent much time with other women before and this was 24/7 with sixty-eight of the best of the best from the bottom of the barrel, including myself!

Are you afraid that you're writing checks your body can't cash? Are you caught up in something that keeps getting worse as time goes on? Do you feel like God is telling you to get out? Have you alienated friends or family because of poor life decisions? Are you afraid or worried a lot of the time?

Lord, help me to see the dangers in life before I am caught right in the middle of them. As I go forth, please close doors that need to be closed and open doors that need to be opened and give me the strength and ability to see the right choices to make. Please have your angels guide and protect me as I boldly go forth.

WHEN YOU ARE READY TO CONFRONT THE WRECKAGE OF YOUR PAST, PRAY, PRAY AND THEN PRAY SOME MORE... THEN BOLDLY STEP OUT IN FAITH!

I was fortunate to have a probation officer that took the time to get to know me and I genuinely knew he liked me and cared about my future. Unfortunately, he and I both knew of the corruption with the criminal justice system at a local level and I knew his help could only extend so far.

After the kidnapping and my rescue, I started over with nothing. I was happy though and within about six months, I had bought a car and got my license squared away. I was epileptic by this time and had some issues regarding my ability to drive safely.

I knew that if I got pulled over and the officer ran my plates and license he would know I was a fugitive and if it was anything like the last time I would be thrown to the ground and handcuffed before there was any conversation. This fear grew worse as more time went by and I finally called my probation officer to surrender myself to the authorities. I was willing to do whatever time the judge felt I deserved for fleeing the state and not contacting anyone as well as not paying the rest of my fine and running out on the people who were trying to get me to roll over on my husband and his contacts.

I arranged to fly back and attend court the day after I got there. My PO wrote a letter to the judge and I was clean and sober with letters from my employer, my pastor, and my landlord. I looked significantly different as well. I stayed with the man who rescued me from the hell I was in and he was concerned that I was going to be sentenced to at least five years in prison. I knew it was going to be prison time as opposed to county time because the last time I went in front of a judge he was sure to tell me that if I screwed up again it would not be county time I was looking at serving. I knew it was going to be thirteen months at least.

I wore a suit to court the next morning and I was the first case on the docket because every second I was in that town was dangerous to my continued health. The judge took his sweet time reading all the documents I brought with me as well as reading the letter from my Probation Officer.

Bob made a mistake on my letter. He recommended revocation of my probation instead of termination. One was bad and one was good. I knew he meant termination because he knew where I lived now and that it would be impossible to see him. The judge asked me about the matter and I explained what I understood to be the intent of the letter.

The judge asked me if I was ready to be remanded into custody and I answered affirmatively. He then asked me if I had a way to leave the state within twenty-four hours if he released me from custody. I again answered affirmatively.

Then he spoke, "After reviewing the case file, the letter from probation, the recommendation of the last judge you appeared in front of and the letters from your current living situation I find you not guilty of the charges against you. It is not my intention to punish the individual that you have fought to become for the person that you were in the past. Your probation is terminated and you may leave. The only requirement I give you is that you need to leave and do not come back into the county. Good luck and God bless you."

I cried for a long time. Then I got on a plane and left. I have never gone back and I abandoned the $100,000 in property that the police department seized on the day I walked out of that house for the last time. I only had two small bags but I left with absolutely nothing except my life and I knew it was a gift from God. The police ransacked the house and removed a ton of stuff, including thirty-six guns and a whole bunch of diamonds. It felt dangerous and stupid to try to recover the few things I thought I needed to start a new life. I had already started over and while I did not have much, what I did own I had earned legally and without causing pain to anybody.

Are you ready to lose the baggage from your past? Have you prayed about the timing and situation that you will find yourself in? Have you made amends with others you have harmed in the past? Is your decision going to cause someone else to be harmed?

Lord, help me to do the right thing at the right time and in the correct manner!! Amen!!

Random Thoughts: A Spiritual Journey

We give and we take
We love and we hate
It is not our fate
It is the choices that we make
  Written by: Michael T. Coe (Audio_Bomb)

***

I would conquer the entire world just to possess you
but once the globe is gently cradled in my triumphant
hands, then you would eventually find my imperfections
& between my fingers you would still slowly slip
through.

Written by: Michael T. Coe (Audio_Bomb

***

It was always her world

It was just a drop of rain

In her flood of emotions

One spectator in the arena

That proclaimed her victory

I was just another burnt out star

In a sky sprinkled with diamonds

Written by: Michael T. Coe (Audio_Bomb

Take the plunge into me just one lunge & you will see a universe to discover, an infinite love in each other.

Written by: Michael T. Coe (Audio_Bomb

IT'S ALL ABOUT THE LOVE!

I have read the Bible often throughout the years and it seems to me that if we follow three of God's laws then all of the commandments fall into line and your character will shine. God tells us to:

Love Him, Love ourselves and Love others! So really, it's all about love. It's real love though. I am referring to action that is unconditional and nonjudgmental as well as love that endures through anger and disappointment. It's loving when you are tired, hungry, cranky, sick, hormonal, stressed and all the other bad feelings and situations that crop up as we go merrily through life trudging the road of happy destiny.

One of the things that helped me become more loving and accepting of everyone I meet is that I really make an effort to pay attention. I watch what people do, what they say, and just as importantly, what they don't do. You can learn a lot about a person's moral compass when you discover what they will not participate in and what they will step into to stop wrong things from happening.

I worked in the grocery industry for years and I was surprised initially to notice that people don't especially use good manners while they are trying to do their entire weekly shopping on their lunch hour, or after work before they go home when all they really want to do is go home and relax a bit. I try to be aware of people that may need some help, and I try to stay out of the way. Grocery aisles aren't as wide as they used to be. I imagine that happened when we went from two kinds of mustard to twenty and BBQ sauce and salad dressing started to take up the best part of an aisle and don't even get me started on cereal!

If a woman is digging in her purse for change I try to just pay the dollar or two she needs.

I wish I could claim this idea as my own but I had someone help me out like that and it was such a blessing. It's a little thing that can mean so much to someone in financial distress, and honestly that's a reality for way to many of us. A majority of the working people in the USA are less than two paychecks from bankruptcy. That situation is like hanging onto a lifeline that is unraveling.

My Grandma lives in Las Vegas; they have a large homeless population as well as professional panhandlers, and she has a huge and generous heart. She takes money with her when she goes out and she gives a small amount to ten people and then she is done for the day. Many folks don't give money away, my mom is one of those, but she will go into the store and buy some food and give it away. It isn't really about giving enough cash so that you may be contributing to a drug or alcohol problem, but it is a kindness and I know that ninety-nine percent of the time it is genuinely appreciated.

Tithing is also an important thing to do as a way to give back your blessings. You will find that if you are faithfully tithing when you think you cannot afford it, the time will come when you can afford it, and even more, you will realize that you can't afford not to. It's a part of being obedient as a Christian. When I don't have an income, I tithe of what I do have: time, clothing and whatever else I can do to fill a need. As a young teenager, I cleaned our church before services. The Bible tells us to cast our bread upon the water, and it will come back to us pressed down, shaken together and running over and if there is one thing I have learned for sure is that you cannot out-give God. He also directs us to give quietly and not to seek out human approval and that giving without attention-seeking will be rewarded in Heaven.

Do you find yourself holding back on giving? Is it the fear that you won't have enough? Have you worked at being as loving as you can be at all times? Have you felt the still, small voice of God directing your giving and tithing?

Lord, I want to be obedient in all things! Please guide my efforts that they may find favor with you and put the people into my life that you want me to bless with a giving spirit.

I PRAYED AND PRAYED & ASKED GOD TO HELP AND HE DIDN'T ANSWER ME. AM I DOING IT WRONG?

I pondered this issue often in my early years as a Christian and it is one of the metaphors that made things that are going to make up the tapestry of our lives. When you look at a large tapestry, the backside doesn't always match the front and yet when the tapestry is turned over it is beautiful and the story is easy to see. I can't even pretend to know what is in the future for me but I trust that as long as I am striving to follow his commandments, he will watch over me. In the past, I would pray about boyfriends, drugs, and all the things that caused me so much anguish and it often seemed as though he didn't even hear my prayers. I was reading the book of Matthew one night and it tells us one of the ways to pray.

Our Father, who art in Heaven, hallowed be thy name. Thy kingdom come, thy will be done, in earth as it is in Heaven. Give us this day our daily bread and forgive us our trespasses as we forgive those who trespass against us. Lead us not into temptation but deliver us from evil, for thine is the kingdom and the power and the glory. Amen.

There are references regarding prayer throughout the Bible and I encourage you to look them up and see that we actually have a fair amount of instruction about the subject.

I pray about pretty much everything and oftentimes it not difficult to know what God wants me to do in the situation I'm bringing before him. It's similar to the way I felt as a kid when I knew what I was thinking about doing would cause me pain and anguish if I was unfortunate enough to be caught.

During my extended stay at kidnapping warehouse, I prayed a lot and even though that was the hardest thing I have had to endure, I always felt like God was right there next to me. In fact, the man that rescued me developed a relationship with the Lord because he saw me pray often and I was amazingly calm considering the insanity going on around me.

While Tony was saving us we drove hair- raisingly fast for almost one-hundred miles until we outran the folks following on our tail. Not long after that, we were pulled over for speeding, not a big surprise, but my rescuer was remanded on an old warrant he wasn't even aware of. The miracles just kept happening.

The police gave me the car and stopped searching for more reasons to arrest Tony. I hadn't driven a car since my adventure began and I was hungry, dehydrated, broke and exhausted. I was also under the influence of whatever they were drugging me with and the final big deal was that I had some crank in my shoe and was of course on probation so it would have been really bad all the way around for me. I was ninety minutes away from safety with no money, it was two am and all I knew about the place I found myself in was that it was closest to a town called Temple.

I went to a payphone and called my parents who had no idea where I was or what happened to me. I told them where I was and the situation and my mom asked me to call her back in ten minutes. I was starting to fade in and out because the adrenaline was finally bleeding off and the shock was setting in with bells on. I called back and my mom told me my sister's husband's parents lived in Temple and would pick me up momentarily and let me use their couch for the night and in the am my parents would drive up and bring me home.

It was a miracle! I only have one sister and one brother and they both lived out of state. I knew almost nobody outside of the place I had lived for the last eight years. I was almost thirty years old and I was grateful to be alive but I could not talk about it and I could not cry until eight months ago. Something shifted in my relationship with God and things started to fall into place and the healing began.

Are you still hurting from something that happened to you in the past? Are you ready to be done hurting and begin to turn your scars into stars? Are you still holding on to things in the past that you know you need to let go? Do you turn it over to God only to take it back as soon as you feel anger and fear?

Lord, help me to remember that you are the Creator and that you know everything that I will potentially face and you have promised never to give me more than I can handle. I claim that promise and know that my healing will happen as long as I continue to stay close to you. Thank you for the gifts of mercy and grace.

THERE ARE FOUR WORDS IN THE ENGLISH LANGUAGE THAT SHOULD BE RETIRED!

I have noticed that people are far less precise with their word choices than they seem to have been in the past. I struggle with this because I hear them all the time and have used them for many years but I am trying to be more authentic and original when I am talking or writing to someone. I sit down with the way I feel and try out different words to see what is appropriate and honest.

My four words that should be retired are Love, Hate, Always, and Never. Did you guess any of them?

I hear the words I love you so often and I admit I am always grateful but I also find myself asking if the person proclaiming love knows what love really is. When I was in High School saying I love you was a big deal but we were teenagers and our feelings were so strong it felt like we had to proclaim them from the mountaintops. Dating as an adult, those words were like gold and the first time you said it there was a huge pause while your man was deciding if he was going to say I love you too. Nowadays it seems to be almost a salutation or term of endearment.

Hate is a very big word and conveys the worst way I can possibly imagine feeling about someone except maybe homicidal. It's also become so common that it has lost the punch that true hatred possesses. I can remember actually physically recoiling from someone shouting I hate you to a friend of mine. It encompasses contempt, disgust, disdain, bitterness, rage, and a desire to cause pain to another person's spirit. Perhaps it's so difficult for me to hear because I have experienced hatred for another child of God and it saddens me in a very private place in my memory palace.

Always and never are easier to discuss because it's simple. The words are usually lies! It is quite an accomplishment to be able to say I have always hated lima beans, but other than that, there just aren't that many absolutes in everyday life. Never is a bit easier because there are thousands of things I have never done or never tried. I've never robbed a bank or gone skydiving! It is one of those words that is used incorrectly unintentionally.

Are you cognizant of the word choices you make? Can you go for a day or a week using different words to express your love? Seriously though, I could just be a bit neurotic about this subject. I used to say I'd rather be hit physically than endure a vitriolic, contemptuous diatribe. Words try to dig inside of a person and erode the joy and self-esteem every child of God deserves to know as a certainty is true. God made me and He doesn't make junk.

You are a beautiful child of God and he created you in his image. Claim your joy and believe in your beauty. IF you don't, who will?

LET ME INTRODUCE YOU TO MY DAD!

My father is a quiet man. He isn't shy or overly introverted and it took me a long time to realize that he doesn't see a reason for small talk very much. He can chat with just about anyone but he doesn't. I have dedicated myself to listening to my dad and learning his stories and the things he has seen and done. Years ago I would have said he was aloof and disinterested but I would have been wrong. A bit at a time, I am getting to know him and the things that he values are the same thing that I value and that's a gift to me. He actually listens very closely and absorbs the information without any big expressions or exclamations. He isn't voluble or loquacious and he doesn't bloviate or disseminate.

When I asked why he was so quiet he told me that a lot of people talk without thinking or don't listen well because they are already trying to frame an answer or comment to interject into the fray. They hear without listening and act without caution. Why impart hard-earned wisdom when folks aren't going to learn that way. I would say he is economic with words, not at all wasteful, and he doesn't verbally recycle but he actually cares quite deeply and his serene calm has helped reach a good place inside when I think things are falling down all around me. He is one of my heroes, and that's as it should be.

When I think about God as my father I naturally think of the things my dad has done throughout my life to teach me something or to protect me from something. The first time I was held at gunpoint was on my seventeenth birthday. I was abducted from out in front of my house woke up to someone knocking on my bedroom window. It was two people I knew and they were both drunk and the big dude had a .357 that he used to encourage me into his truck.

He told me they were going to take me into the desert, rape me, and then shoot me. He informed me that he didn't care if his lover had casual sex with someone else but he would not tolerate a time out from their relationship while his man ran around with me.

This was all new information for me. I had been aware that Ron, the guy I was dating, was bi-sexual but I didn't know his lover was on steroids, an alcoholic, and apparently very jealous. I learned from this adventure that getting in the middle of someone's relationship can be dangerous to my continued well-being.

So, I finally got away and I had to hurt them to do it, and I managed to make my way back home where I promptly went into shock and couldn't stop shaking or crying. My parents came out to see what was wrong, they decided to wait until morning to address the issue, and we went to bed.

My dad took less than a month to move me to another state along with the rest of my family. He did that to protect me and at significant personal cost to himself and he did it because he is my dad and he loves me. It was not the optimal time to move for several reasons but my parents both decided that it was not safe for me to stay when the men that hurt me had not been apprehended.

Knowing that about my earthly father, I can barely comprehend the level that God, my Father, loves every one of us thousands of times more than our earthly parents can love us. It's an amazeballs feeling to understand that depth of love.

Do you compare your relationship with your dad to your relationship to God, the Father? Have you taken the negative feelings from your family and projected them to God? Can you possibly imagine how much God loves every one of us? It's huge and it's wonderful!

Heavenly Father, thank you for the protection you provide as we go through life striving to live according to your laws. I offer you praise for being the awesome protector that you have always been. You are a refuge from the storm and I love you.

BUT IT'S JUST NOT FAIR!

Life isn't fair and once we pass fifth grade it has probably already shown you the truth of that statement. My boyfriend has a saying that really is the truth of the matter. He says, "I'm not so good at getting out of trouble but I am excellent at not getting into it in the first place."

It pains me but I have to admit that my adventure with kidnap and torture is something I might have avoided if I had taken the time to get to know my husband better before I married him. He had gotten into a bad accident shortly before I met him and a mutual friend introduced me to him. I am a masseuse and he really needed a significant amount of help because his pain was very bad and his mobility was virtually at a standstill.

I started out working on his neck and shoulders and he was a sweetheart. He was soft spoken, patient, and not at all difficult to look at or talk to. Everything was just so easy and comfortable. I moved in with him and his mother after two months. They were both very loving and kind, I lost my job and couldn't afford my rent, and it seemed like a perfect solution.

We got married four months later. The day after we got married everything changed. I should have left back then but it wasn't all bad and my husband's paralysis turned out to be permanent. I felt sorry for both of them and thought they needed me to survive, never thought about what they did before I met them. The changes in both of them were astounding.

His mom started out by letting his caretaker go, saying that I could clean the house and take care of my husband's physical therapy. She then started to berate me for everything I did that didn't make her happy. She began to wake me up earlier and earlier to get started on the day's work. I have always loved to read and she gave me unending grief about it until I began to read late at night by flashlight under the covers. My husband's sweet generosity ended like it had never occurred in the first place. I had to clean exactly the way she wanted and that's probably why I rebelled once I was out of that situation. She hid my things from me and then said she hadn't seen them. I was forbidden to put any of my personal belongings anywhere in the house. It all had to go in the attic.

My husband promised me we would move out as soon as we got married. He lied. He was still sweet for the most part but he began to hide money from me and wanted me to use my money for the things we needed. I never got a birthday or Christmas present, which isn't a huge deal, but it hurt. His friends began to come over and I learned that he was part of a group that demanded allegiance and his job was to enforce their edicts. Everyone thought because he was in a wheelchair that he was harmless but it only takes one finger to squeeze a trigger. He made me sell my car because he had two and I wasn't encouraged to go anywhere without him. When we started our business, we used the money from my car.

After years of pain and turmoil, I knew it was time to go. I was going to die or kill someone if I had to endure much more. When I tried to leave, he called the police and told them he was paralyzed and I had access to guns and he was fearful for his life. When I tried to escape, he took everything I wanted to take with me including all the jewelry I was wearing and the shoes off my feet.

I'm not saying I deserved everything that happened to me but if I had taken the time to really get to know him, perhaps I would have made a different decision. If I had left when things got so terrible, I would have avoided a lot of heartache. I was afraid to leave because he threatened to kill me if I ever tried to leave. If I hadn't started doing crank to keep up with the demands on my time maybe I would have weighed more than ninety-four pounds when I finally left. My choice to use drugs rather than get out and get better haunts me.

Are you in a situation that is untenable? Are you abused and think you deserve it? Are you afraid for your life? Do you think you can't afford to leave?

There are always solutions to the problems we face. It may take some creative thinking and time but you do not have to stay in an abusive relationship. There are counselors to talk to, ways to earn money on line, and if you have kids it's much more harmful to let them see abuse than to learn to live with a single parent.

BE THE BEST YOU IT'S POSSIBLE TO BE!

I know I said sex introduced in a relationship too early causes issues down the line but kissing is important to most people. After the initial physical attraction, whether or not your partner can turn you on is important. Some people don't feel as strongly about it as I do but I would say the majority think it's a big deal.

Of course, you can always teach your partner the way you like to kiss and vice versa. Communication is obviously a key part of any relationship. I know people who have a high sex drive and they fall for someone that either has a low sex drive or even none at all. I believe that I would have a hard time not finding someone else to fill that need in my life. I don't cheat on my man but I could see resentment building up over time.

I am also a very affectionate person and I know that's very important to me. It may even be more important than the sex. I have been in a relationship where sex and affection were completely cut off after a couple of years. I know that as a relationship loses that warm, fuzzy desire to have sex daily, but time seems to create a situation where sex doesn't happen as often. I wonder if it's because people know that if they don't have sex tonight they can have it tomorrow or the next day and before you know it you find yourself too tired or to stressed and then it becomes less spontaneous until it's something that almost has to be scheduled.

If you want to keep that spark alive, both people have to make an effort to be sexy and romantic. A friend of mine said that between her kids, their activities and her job, she could see herself letting things slide. She stopped dressing nicely and they tried to set up a date night but life happens when we have to deal with lots of other things. I have another friend who laments that his wife completely let her appearance deteriorate until she was wearing sweats all the time and she stopped putting on make-up and doing her hair. I know several women that said they would get in the mood more often if their men would do something like the dishes or laundry, anything to give her fifteen minutes to relax. My man used to have a hot bath ready for me when I got home from work and I can't even express how wonderful and thoughtful that gesture is.

People define romance in a variety of ways. Some women prefer a nice dinner and maybe some flowers while others believe that if their partner supports them emotionally, protects them from harm, and helps without begging, they feel like they won the lottery. My boyfriend is not a heart, flowers, or anniversary person but he has allowed me to stay home and write, and he is so supportive in every way. I think that is amazing and quite romantic.

Have you stopped trying to look your best if you're not going out anywhere? Do you support your partner and encourage his/her dreams? Are you affectionate and complimentary? What can you do to show your partner your romantic side?

Lord, help me to be the best mate that I can and remind me to be grateful and to show him/her that they are a blessing in my life. Make me an instrument of your peace.

IT IS NOT OUR ABILITIES THAT SHOW THE MEASURE OF AN INDIVIDUAL AS MUCH AS IT'S THE CHOICES WE MAKE.

I know many people with aspirations, ambition, and dreams of being successful and wealthy so that they can retire at forty but I don't know many that have the discipline and drive to put in the time to get their dreams realized. Television doesn't help in this due to reality shows that reward folks for just about anything. They even have shows that try to find the perfect match for the person being showcased. My problem with these shows is that they gives the contestants as well as the male or female searching for their soul mate a completely unrealistic picture of what each person is truly like. It's akin to Cinderella at the ball. They get to travel to exotic places and eat amazing food and they don't have to work. If you can't be fun, charming, and thoughtful in that situation there's something wrong. What about how your dream man handles loss, pain or anger?

I have the ability to write well and I know it and believe it to be true. I didn't have the time or inclination to actually create an outline and then write a book. I was also a bit short on ambition and I had bunches of obstacles to overcome. When I shifted my focus and began to see the glass as half full the blessings began.

Due to having a stroke fifteen years ago, my memory can be a challenge but writing this book has been amazing. I use flashcards to explain the basic concept I want each entry to impart. The format is easy to follow and the next book will probably be a fictionalized story that resembles the insanity of my life. I made a decision to spend time writing every day. It was really interesting to learn that, although I had a hard time even thinking about keeping each person straight and developing a city for the characters to live in and making sure that if someone died or ended up in the hospital, I didn't have them running around shooting the bad guys so I found ways to compensate.

I also learned that I can write decent poetry and I developed discipline by writing every day and posting them on Instagram and that turned out to be awesome. I have a writing group on Instagram that is just amazeballs. They are supportive and funny and offer great ideas.

Most people are blessed with talent and finding out what that talent is can take you places you never dreamed. There are programs on the internet that test you to see what kind of job you'd be good at. You spend a third of your life at work so it's kind of important that you enjoy what you do.

The only thing we truly have control over is the way we react (the choices we make) to the things that happen every day. Just because you feel something, that doesn't mean your first reaction should be giving into the feelings and doing something irreparable.

I made choices that led down the path that ended with my kidnapping. I am not saying I deserved it any way but I can see the poor decisions I made that were a precursor to a lot of pain. Being compulsive is a character defect I have, and it is still with me. I was not coerced. Guilt and shame live inside me because of bad choices made on impulse.

Are your choices impulsive and made during times you are very emotional? Can you try to avoid situations that are fraught with bad choices? Are you ready to learn how to control your feelings? Are you ready to make healthy choices for yourself?

Lord, help me to hear your still, small voice when I am about to make bad choices. I know I have the mind of Christ and the right actions and decisions are there for me if I take the time to listen.

IF YOUR PET AND A STRANGER WERE DROWNING AND YOU COULD ONLY SAVE ONE OF THEM, WHICH ONE WOULD YOU SAVE?

Initially this seems like a no brainer question but I have met many people whose pets are like their children. Personally, I would pull a Captain Kirk and change the rules. I would tell the stranger to hold onto my cat as if his life would depend on it. A good friend of mine asked me if the individual was a stranger or a friend and said she would make her decision according to that answer. That was before I used the word stranger and just said a person.

I thought it was a simple decision because humans have souls but that was before my beloved cat lived for twenty-seven years and always gave me a ton of love. When he died, I thought my heart had been cut out. I believe that animals have souls and I understand that many people don't believe that and that's ok. It took me far longer to recover from his death but I believe he's in Heaven or maybe cat Heaven.

I have had friends and family that have passed away including a brother-in-law that I adored and a cousin that I was close to but I have not had someone that lived in my house die. That event caused me to be more thoughtful and grateful for the people I am close to and I make a real effort to tell them I love them and specifically to express the things about them that I cherish.

I now have two rescue cats and they are six years old now as well as siblings although my girl is a bit feral and skittish. My boy climbs in my lap while I read or watch TV and if I move from one room to another he follows me. He weighs twenty-four pounds and is a very long and tall cat, not an obese one. I know everyone doesn't feel that way about their pets and I understand that perspective because I have had pets throughout most of my life and while I enjoyed and took good care of them it pales in comparison to the way I currently feel about my babies.

Do you have pets? Are you taking good care of them? Are you too busy to take care of your pet? Do you know that your pets depend on you and in exchange, they provide love and affection without nagging or going on a shopping expedition? Are you neglecting their basic needs?

Lord, help me to best take care of my pets and if I am too busy help me to find a good home for them. I know you care about all creatures, big and small because in your word it says that you care for the birds in the trees and how much more do you care for us.

TOO MUCH & NOW IT'S TOO LATE

I ache to return to yesterday.
I'd change the things I said.
I'd hide the disgust and disappointment on my face,
I hope you would see the love I possess for you &
I see everything.
I know that you are busting your butt,
Giving 110% to the effort
While I have detached
And coldly sit in judgment.
I know I need to alter my focus,
To be the supportive partner that you need,
But you can't unshoot a gun
Any more than you can unspeak words.
and it feels like I'm choking on the fear
That this is just the beginning
Of an ugly ending.

When the people we love say cruel and venomous things it pierces like a blade and the first thing to explore is whether this is something you can deal with or if it seems to be getting worse and there doesn't seem to be an end in sight.

If you respond in the same tone things can escalate very quickly and I promise that they will get out of hand and words may be said in the heat of the moment that are not true; or have a degree of truth but most of it is misplaced anger or fear. Everyone is capable of just losing it.

WHAT HAPPENS WHEN WE ADD
ALCOHOL TO THE PROBLEM?

In a drunken rage I broke one boyfriend's jaw, cracked a rib fighting a stranger, and I could not control myself when I was drinking. After those incidents I was aware that alcohol in excess was not my friend and I didn't know how to drink without getting drunk. I also said things I didn't mean, or worse, I told other people's secrets and there's no excuse for that. All the anger I usually held inside bubbled over when alcohol was present.

There are scores of references in the Bible urging people not to be drunkards and it goes one further and says not to hang out with them either. This does not mean that we don't minister to them. Sometimes a drunk gets that way because of trauma, abuse or a chemical imbalance in the brain or body. I know people that hate themselves because they drink and they are so sincere until it's time to quit. They try repeatedly and every time they relapse, the self-hatred grows. Alcoholism is a disease and it wants to kill.

I have had people around me, people that I love a great deal, get to the point where drinking is the only thing that matters. It fuels the desire to be as hedonistic as possible. I certainly let my desire for oblivion win out over friends and family during the last months of my power drinking. I was not treating my body as a temple. It was closer to a public bathroom (ok, it wasn't really that bad but it was bad enough for me to hit bottom) and I had no self-respect and once I got sober I saw some of my drinking buddies; and I thought their brains were scrambled.

At one point, someone very close to me fell in love with the Pentecostal church and was cured and delivered from the disease of alcoholism. It was ok at first but before long she was drinking pretty much any time of the day or night and she was not a happy drunk. She was strident and suspicious and accused me of many things I didn't even understand. She drank at home and made the household feel like walking on eggshells. I felt like I was run over by a car, and then the car went into reverse and ran over me again. In the am, she had almost no recall of the previous day and the horrible things that she said.

We all managed to survive the tempest, and we are all sober and still close. There really is redemption and God has infinite grace and mercy. We, as his children, can be graceful and merciful as well. Human beings have an amazing capacity for forgiveness.

Are you doing things you know are hurting those you love the most? Do you have addictive behavior about anything in your life? Do you realize many of us just switch one addiction to another and try to convince others that now that you are done with drugs, alcohol, casual sex, smoking or food just to name a few.

Father God, I am baring my soul and ask that you take this compulsion from me. I willingly give it up so that I may draw stronger with you and make amends to those that were torn apart by my actions. I will do whatever is necessary so that I may once again feel the peace that surpasses all understanding.

DENIAL ISN'T ONLY A RIVER IN EGYPT

Outbound train!

Come one, come all

Step right up to the train "Denial"

Patiently waiting for quite a while

You crossed paths as a child

Then again as a teen

She didn't mind waiting

She's as patient as she seems

You can lie, cheat and steal

Denial will hide the way you feel

Drink and do dope,

Forget to grow up

Denial will tell you

Everything's fine, just don't give up hope.

Denial often is hard to see because of the nature of the beast. It can sneak up on you and before you know it you're knee deep in muck with nobody to lend a hand and help you out. Some denial allows us to cope with some of the more traumatic moments in life. The brain can blur just about anything if your first look at something is traumatic. It won't keep you from seeing it forever, but that first look scrambles everything.

85

We can be in denial about work, our relationships, our health and the list goes on. I had a very difficult time admitting I was addicted to pain pills. My rationalization was that my doctor was writing the prescriptions so it must have been okay to take them. I never admitted that I had two doctors at all times giving me duplicate prescriptions and when I ran out I would go to an urgent care or emergency room. I can admit today that it took almost all my time to keep myself stocked with meds. I only see one doctor and use one pharmacy nowadays. It's healthier for me all around.

I have been in denial over relationships, including marriage. I had a man give me to another man less than six months into our relationship and I can say unequivocally that I should have walked out then even though I was scared and alone and could barely afford it; I still should have walked. Any love I may have had for him died at that moment.

I also had a man try to kill me and there were some warning signs that I should have seen. I should have known that there was no way the situation was going to improve. The first one was when he refused to move out after we got married and then I really got an education when he was welcomed back into his organization like the prodigal son. We spent the first night with these guys making silencers for guns that they were selling. I actually had someone show up at the door one night to "borrow" a gun. Who does that? I gave him the gun after I cleaned it and loaded the clips with gloves on. I was also very specific when I told him that if he had to use it I never wanted to see it again.

Much later I would be grateful that nobody paid attention to me because one of our guns was used to kill a police officer who was undercover and that proved to be the kiss of death for two of the folks we knew. I wasn't afraid every day. I knew I wouldn't be able to survive the experience unless I learned how to compartmentalize all the things I saw and did as well as the nightmares I heard about. I did that with such success that after it was all over I never shed a tear, never threw a fit and never grieved.

Finally, seven months ago, I was on the phone with my mom and I got a huge info dump that gave me pictures of what happened, dialogue of things that were said to terrify me, and lots of random stuff that didn't make sense to me at the time. I started to cry, I could hear her crying as well, and I asked her why she was upset.

She said, "You have been carrying this around with plywood barriers put up in front of the details and now you are strong enough to see some of what happened and to choose to let it go." She sounded more emotional than I have heard in a long time. I realized that during those forty-five days she had no idea where I was, if I was alive, and if I was ever going to surface again. She's a therapist and has worked with lots of people who have seen and survived shootings and other traumatic events but I am her daughter and she didn't have any professional distance from my own personal train wreck.

Are you hiding from your own tragedy? Do you have periods that you can't account for? Do you find yourself drinking, drugging or having sex in order to medicate through the pain? Have you asked God to restore your mind and spirit?

We are all in denial but eventually all the walls come down and we pray for the strength of the serenity prayer: God grant me the serenity to accept the things I cannot change, the courage to change the things I can and the wisdom to know the difference.

ARE YOU DEALING WITH AN EATING DISORDER, OR DEPRESSION, OR SELF-HARMING?

I have a friend who was really battling all the things that teens and young adults face in these media saturated times that we find ourselves participating in. She had bulimia, depression and she was a cutter. She was beginning to get involved in other ways to fill the bottomless void that dwelt inside. The thing I am most amazed about is that these beautiful people all seem to think they are fat. Fat in places where there is no fat. It boggles the mind but they are sincere and so I recognize the fact that self-esteem is intrinsically bound to their perceptions and body image. I tried the practical and logical solution of pulling her in front of a mirror and asked her to show me what she was talking about. She obviously did not see the same thing I did in the mirror.

The following note is one I wrote to her when she was really suffering:

Hi babes, I want you to know that you are in my thoughts and prayers nightly. I used to feel the exact same things you do except you have to deal with the internet and other forms of social media. Someone can post a letter full of lies with a picture that isn't even of you that has been photo-shopped and it can go around the world and be viral in almost no time at all. That makes things even more complicated.

When it comes to pictures take the safe and easy way out. Do not allow anyone to ever take a picture of you that you wouldn't want your entire family to see proudly posted in the nooks and crannies of the Internet. There are bunches of reasons to avoid this trap and not many at all that have any kind of positive outcome.

I was constantly full of rage and self-righteous indignation along with deep disappointment with everyone but mostly I was disappointed with myself. I had rigidly high expectations about everything. Being a teenager and young adult is an emotional time.

I have some simple suggestions that might help and you are always welcome to contact me or your pastor or whoever is in your life that knows how precious you are and sees you struggling for a way to just exist without the pain.

Sooo…to feel better: drink a ton of water (at least 64 ounces a day), instead of trying to eat large meals have something every four or five hours and try to make these snacks high in protein, low in fat and sugar but keep them uncomplicated and small so the urge to throw up isn't as overwhelming.

Realize that life is cyclical so whatever you let into your heart and mind is the same thing that will beg for expression in return. If I listen to music that is angry and full of negative lyrics, I discover that my attitude or views are negative. There is a saying that fits the subject here and it's GIGO (Garbage in, Garbage out). It isn't always like that but I do find that if I temper the input of information does affect the output.

Make small goals that are not impossible to achieve and this will help you feel better about yourself. I was about ten or fifteen pounds overweight. I have never been obese but it has been a challenge to lose the last seven pounds. My problem is that I was anorexic for decades and every time I looked in the mirror, a fat chick was right there in the glass. I recently discovered that food is good and so the old me that never really even got liked food has decided food is a good thing. Make sure that as you complete the small tasks you reward yourself for a job well done.

Start a journal and write down when you have so much taking up space in your heart and mind that you feel like you are going to vomit feelings all over the place. Keep on writing until you feel a bit empty and a bit more peaceful. Don't lie to yourself; it doesn't help at all.

When it comes to self-harming, I have first-hand experience. The big difference from me doing it in the 1970's and someone doing it today is that it is much more widespread and it's a way for a teen who feels like they have no control over things to feel a measure of control. It allowed me to feel the pain of cutting, I got satisfaction from bleeding, and it was a secret that my parents knew nothing about. It's like having a broken hand and wanting someone to stomp on your feet so you have something different to focus on. Instagram has many people that are in recovery from self-harming and they are a very caring and thoughtful group of people who are always willing to listen if you need to vent or just talk for a bit.

It may sound a little lame but it's important to fill your time to see what's available within your community, either at a school or community center. There is always a need for volunteers at all kinds of businesses and there are all kinds of information and classes available online. Helping others always benefits you too. My dad did some collecting for a while. He did coins, then stamps. I found the stamps to be interesting.

Are you self-harming and feel like it's getting out of control? Do you think there are better ways to deal with the things that occur in your life than your current solutions? Do you binge and purge with food, trying to fill up a hole inside you that can't be filled that way? Are you suicidal or thinking of suicide? Do you have someone older you can trust to talk to when you feel overwhelmed? Please make a list of hotline numbers that allow you to talk whenever you want and you can be anonymous if you feel like it.

Father God, Please place your angels to protect and guide our kids when we aren't able to be there. Please let them feel the part of you that is inside each one of us.

WHY DO WE ALWAYS HURT THE ONES WHO LOVE US THE MOST?

The basic consensus seems to be that we are aware that the ones who love us the most are not going to disappear if we stop being one of the happy shiny people. An old boyfriend used to ask me how I could spend my entire day dealing with difficult customers and always have nice, calm and kind words for them but when I got home I'd vent and pick on him constantly. Sadly, there's some truth to this.

When we get done working for the day and arrive home we want to relax, unwind, eat, relax some more and sleep. Sometimes we may have had a really crappy day and had to suck it up and keep quiet so we don't become unemployed and when we get home it all just dribbles out. Feelings of frustration, unappreciation, and fatigue can affect even the sweetest folks. I used to snipe and yell for five or ten minutes and then calm down. Now I can let the emotion go on my way home. I picture myself dropping all my anxiety out the window like litter. If it's been a super bad day I take a bath when I get home to try to release more of the tension. Finally, I remember to focus on the many beautiful traits that the people I love share and the last thing I want to do is take out misplaced anger on someone I love.

My customers are strangers and it is my job to pleasantly take care of their problems in an expeditious manner. It is not a hardship to be kind to people who are being kind to me. The occasional customer that gets out of line, swears, or threatens lets me know that I am not his problem. Nothing I have said or done warrants that type of overreaction and for the most part I let them vent for a short time and then I go back to doing my job of fixing their problems calmly and nicely. I am also aware that I am being paid to perform that function.

I was in a wheelchair, on crutches, or in braces for a fair amount of time over the years so I'm very sensitive to people that are disabled or in some other way needing a bit of help. My husband was paralyzed and he needed help with a multitude of things that we take for granted every day so I became super aware of things I could do that would allow him to care for himself and that really helped him feel more like a functional part of the family instead of a constant burden.

After I had a stroke, I saw a completely different side to life. I'm not sure of the reasons why but I promise this really happened to me a lot of the time. I would be making my way through the grocery store slowly and when I would stop to look at something in order to make a decision a well-meaning person would walk up to me and raise their voice into almost a yell and ask me if I needed help. I confess I didn't see the correlation between handicapped and deaf or blind but it served as a cute and sweet thing to do so I always just smiled and asked for the help I needed.

Another reason it's so easy to get along with strangers is that there is no relationship between them and me and no history that causes resentment or overreaction. The more history you have with someone the more apt you are to assign hidden motives to their words and actions and sometimes we do that without even realizing it.

I used to do that with my mom all the time because in the very distant past she used to say unkind things in a very condescending voice. It made me see red. It's probably fair to say I was unhappy before she even opened her mouth. I knew what she was going to say and how she was going to say it and I probably had the same tendencies. It's a self-fulfilling prophecy.

Now we have a great time together and I wish she was closer because she's a great person. She is smart, loving, nurturing, fun and encouraging. My parents will be married 50 years this year and I am proud at the determination and effort that went into a good marriage and allowed them to be good parents.

One of the things that really helped me is to separate the words from the voice. Maybe the person you are talking to is super annoyed at someone else but you walked up and started a conversation and now the other person has to realize they are annoyed but not with the person in front of them and it's not as easy as you'd think to successfully mask emotion and switch gears right in the middle.

Do you use and angry or disrespectful tone of voice a lot with people? Is it their fault that you feel the way you do or are you carrying emotion from something else and venting with someone who it's safe to yell at? Can you make an effort to do one thing for me? When someone raises their voice to you, lower your voice in response and see if that lowers the tone of both sides of the conversation. I think you'll be surprised.

Let me be aware as I go through the day to keep my voice low, respectful and pleasant, and it would be good if my face matched my words.

IF YOU STEADFASTLY REFUSE TO QUIT, YOU RAPIDLY NARROW YOUR OPTIONS UNTIL WINNING IS THE ONLY CHOICE LEFT.

This is the way I used to feel about marriage and to be honest I wish I still felt this way but time goes on and we change and adapt to the times and the attitudes of the people around us. When I got married we lived alone in a small town about ninety minutes away from both sets of parents. We both worked and worked hard so we had all of our needs and a fair amount of our wants without going into debt.

We lived in one of the hottest cities in California and we went to visit some friends for a long weekend in the Bay Area. It was love at first sight and, after talking to my husband, we agreed that if I could find a job during the trip we could move to this paradise. I interviewed twice with just one company and I got the job. It was a significant raise and I was going into a field I knew nothing about but I was confident it would be awesome. We moved into our friends kitchen (yes, the kitchen was that big) and my husband got a job right away. We stayed with them for slightly over a month and then we moved into a two bedroom apartment.

Our problems started out small. Little things that were said that should not have been said and thoughtless deeds that were blown way out of proportion on both sides. Everyone wanted to know when we were going to get pregnant. Through a series of events, we learned I couldn't have babies and I believe that issue destroyed something inside me. I tried to get past it and over it and it just became bigger and bigger. We didn't talk about it and maybe if we had, things may have ended differently. I know that I gave up on God because a doctor told me I couldn't conceive.

Then I gave up on my husband because I knew how much he wanted kids and he deserved kids. He was and still is a good man. He married again and has three kids and I think that's awesome but I know now that I gave up almost without a fight because I was just too shocked to deal with it.

I don't give up anymore. I know exactly what I deserve and I know exactly the price Christ paid so I could have favor with God and he told me, "If you delight in Me, I will delight in you and give you the desires of your heart." I have been blessed again and again just because I take that scripture to heart and know that if I hold it there, it will bear fruit. It has in the past, it does right now, and it will continue into the future.

The biggest desire of my heart right now (besides goddaughter, The Sashkah) is to finally write and publish a book. I have been writing since fourth grade and I have started probably fifteen or twenty books but I just can't see them. It's like trying to look through the fog. It's an absolute lesson in futility. It looks like God kept up his side of things because my book comes out next Friday.

Here's the funny part. I started writing poetry on Instagram and I did nothing to try to find followers. It is a labor of love and a way for my goddaughter and her friends to check in with me and I love that they do that. I have an amazing group of folks on Instagram that write amazeballs poetry and we support each other's writing regularly. So, here I am - a poet on Instagram who writes and shares with my friends and one day I decide that I can write a book that is similar to a journal or something to meditate with. I got excited and now it's a reality. Because I didn't give up! Because I did the footwork and researched the things I was curious about and I have the whole thing outlined, which was a huge miracle in and of itself, and it will be ready for publishing in seven days.

Have you given up on your dreams? Have you stopped trying to achieve that better job? Do you want a partner to share your life with but just feel like it's hopeless? Have you given up just before your dreams will be realized?

Lord, thank you for being a God that doesn't break promises. You have a long history of doing what you say you will and being who you say you are. I know that you want to see me achieve the desires of my heart because I can feel it inside of me in the place where I hear your voice speaking to me. Thank you for everything.

I'M OLD ENOUGH TO WORK AND BUY MY OWN STUFF

It's really just a simple truth. Everything that goes up will eventually come down. I remember the first couple of jobs I had with something like tolerant reflection. I did the fast food gig because it was easy, it didn't require a lot of time, or a horrible uniform. I chose places close to my parents' house so I could walk if I had to. I rode a bike or the bus if I didn't catch a drive with a friend or a coworker. I learned the lessons someone entering the workforce assimilates in the early months.

I learned that unless I had a special skill set I was going to start at a new place making minimum wage and doing the grunt work that everybody hated to do. I learned about budgeting money and that was quite an eye-opener. My mom and dad had always made sure that my needs were met but I discovered the difference between needs and wants. I had many wants and some things that I thought were needs turned out to be wants according to my parents.

I figured out the difference between shopping at K-Mart or Target and shopping at Wet Seal or Express and Hot Topic. I learned that sometimes if I took the time and energy to check out all the stores I could get really good deals regardless of where I shop. There is a definite difference in quality from the cheapest stores to the most exclusive but there is a middle of the road just about everywhere and there are different shops that have great buys but you have to have some kind of inside information to figure the whole thing out. I didn't need designer stuff but I didn't want my entire wardrobe to be hand-me-downs or some weird shade of yellow that you can always find on clearance.

My parents did not charge me rent while I was in high school and I could work as long as my grades didn't suffer and my grades never suffered so that wasn't really an issue. After high school, I was no longer having fun at my folk's house and they objected to stuff like me not coming home at night or coming home drunk or stoned. I can see this issue from both sides at this point in life, but when I was eighteen, it seemed really petty so I got a job taking care of two kids and moved in there. I got a job while the kids were in school and I had fun, and money wasn't a big deal but the kids mom was gone for weeks at a time, and that got old quick. I didn't have days off and I was only eighteen and it felt like I got all the responsibilities of having kids with not of the fun of creating them.

Now I'm forty-nine years old and I think my parents are great and I'm grateful that my Gram's is ninety-three and still up and doing her thing and praise the Lord for that. My siblings both live out of state and I wish they were closer, but they aren't and I accept that. My goddaughter is dating for the first time and I think her boyfriend is an amazing kid and she's everything to me so I temper my reaction so I don't come across like a prison warden or the dating police, but I also am very careful not to encourage them to have a lot of unsupervised time. We all had the talk with her and it was hilarious because of how quick her mind is and how embarrassed we were at trying to have the talk in the first place. I marvel at the hormonal shifts and I actually like the music she listens to. She helps me get food on the table but still believes there's a kitchen genie that does all the clean-up and starts the dishwasher.

I have no comparison with cell phones and their abilities. When I was growing up there were no cellular phones. Seriously, there were pagers but not everyone had them and of the young folks that I knew that used those ninety percent of them were drug dealers. I bought my own first car and every car after that until in my forties I had a period of time where my brain wasn't working quite right and working wasn't possible so my parents helped me get a used car, and I was and always will be grateful for their help.

I think I grew up at a good time. We were a normal and close family. My mom made sure we all learned how to cook at least the basics. I enjoy cooking and baking and can do both without disastrous results. I did my fair share of stupid things but stayed out of jail mostly. I was arrested for indecent exposure but I was more afraid of my parents' reaction than the reaction of the police so I ran as fast as I could and got home without more drama.

If we wanted to play with friends we went outside and yelled, whoever felt like playing yelled back, and we met in the center of the street to decide what to play. When the street lights went on it was time to come home. Common sense was prized and naivety was charming. I do know that every generation thinks nobody can possibly understand life as they are forced to live it and there may be a slight amount of truth to that. I can't figure out how kids can figure out every digital/wireless device without having to read a book or take a class. It's amazing and a bit daunting.

Are you a parent of a teenager now? Do you see the differences between now and the generation you grew up in? Did you have everything you wanted and needed or was it different for you? Have you sat down and discussed what you all need versus what we all want? Do you force yourselves to carve out some real family time? You can go bowling, watch a movie, and play cards or games or even just sharing a meal with no phones or TV's on.

Lord, help me to be more in touch with my family. Help me to be more thoughtful and supportive of what the other people in my life are going through. Give me the words to better express my love and approval of everyone in my family.

Angels weep as demons roar & the faithful spend their lives in prayer.It's difficult to explain to those still innocent. However, nothing about this is good or fair. Evil extends temptations galore those that are with them scream out for more! Good men try to protect the flock while the evil ones laugh and mock. Families are falling away we're too busy to pray. Families turn on each other citing imaginary rifts, the righteous cry out in prayer. Inside they feel cast adrift when the progress is measured by a secular yardstick. The meek and the humble feel sick. God is the father but the price is high but Christ died for our sins. We are humanities dirty little secrets. Discarded by those trying so hard to beat us. We are human liter, our shame runs deep, Everlastingly churning through the memories we keep. Animals get rescued but recuing humans doesn't seem to be the goal. We are a rag-tag group of lost little boys and girls, we go into the world to be beat and stay low.

It's difficult to me to get back in the headspace of a homeless or unwanted person. I have certainly walked down that road and have forgotten none of it. The constant cold and never-ending hunger kept me shaky and afraid. I was very scared at night. Usually I broke into someone's RV so I could sleep without being attacked or molested and I was very quiet and stealthy so most people never even knew they gave me shelter when nobody else would.

In the beginning, the police were also looking for me so it became mission critical that I had somewhere to bunk down for the night. I came so close to being caught and arrested that I could hear the officer breathing. I stayed still and quiet and he moved on to check something else that looked suspicious to him. I did eventually face up to the wreckage of my past and I don't wake up screaming as often anymore because I still dream of the worst moments.

I didn't think I had many regrets because I believe that every bad thing I did or had done to me contributed to making me the person I am today, but as I gain more time and distance I realize that I do have some regrets and most of them involve things that caused pain to more than just myself. Stealing the Porsche was kind of a low class thing to do and I kept it for a week. I showed up at my parents' house loaded frequently for many years. I wasn't a good sister or daughter while I was in the midst of my addiction and selfishness. I gave up on myself.

Are you self-medicating to avoid feeling too much of anything? Are you in denial about something that is far more addicting than you are aware of? Have your close relationships fallen to the wayside?

Lord, help me to remember I am a worthy person. I do not have to settle for half a life. You are the great healer and addiction is a disease. Help me to be strong enough to seek help. I know your mercy and grace is sufficient for me.

THE YEARS FLY BY TOO QUICKLY TO SPEND THEM IN SILENT PRISONS OF HATE!

Life has many challenges, everyone goes through tragedy in some form or another, and sadly, most of us are dumped on and treated like crap at least once. I can say this with a fair amount of certainty because I was married to a man that caused me to lose my home, my business and if he'd had his way, my life. I had to start over without even a pair of shoes.

I didn't mean to hold onto the resentment and hate but it was quite a while before I could even really begin to let it go - it stayed in my dreams for years. It was wrong, unfair, and I didn't deserve it but life's not fair and he took too many years from me already and I was determined he wouldn't take any more but it proved to be more difficult than it first appeared.

First, I had to own my part of it and while it wasn't a whole bunch of percentage points that made up the mess, there were certainly things I could have done to minimize my risk and avoid parts of the eventual fallout. I could have waited longer to get engaged, I could have made it a long engagement, I could have said goodbye when everyone broke his or her word. I should have walked out after the drugs became an everyday part of life. I should have tried to leave without my money.

Then I got grabbed off the streets and taken to the place I would spend forty-five days waiting for the day

I would die .My opinion was never solicited although there was certainly plenty of communication. I answered so many rude questions that I stopped trying to figure out why life had gone so horribly wrong. I met many new people during my time in captivity and they all had a lot to say except the ones who didn't talk at all, but they wanted something else from me. I told the truth repeatedly and the few things I lied about became a form of the truth. I knew every day was walking a tightrope straight down to hell.

As time went on things got a little easier. I knew they were never going to open the door and tell me I was free to leave. I wasn't sure exactly how it was all going to end but I had a pretty good idea. Toward the end it got worse. Just like everything else in life, it was darkest before the dawn. I don't know about anyone else but the mind numbing terror inciting fear just isn't sustainable over long periods of time so I settled into a kind of vigilant watching. I suppose I could have done something to force them to kill me but I thought I would end up dead and they would still be breathing and that wasn't successful conflict resolution to me. Call me all kinds of names but if I was going to die it wasn't going to be alone.

At the end, the showdown, the big show, things seemed to slow way down. A man who knew how to kick ass and take names rescued me and with my help and a little help from God, we got out of there. There were fireworks as I left that nasty, damp, warehouse with no bed, no food, no love but forty-four hand grenades and I got my hands on two and that was all they wrote. The chapter ended and I went on with life. I can't say with any real authority what happened to my captors. I have been briefed on the subject and I live a nice and quiet life so I'm thinking the final score was: kidnappers - 0, Jean - 1!

Anyway, I think my own example is a wee bit extreme but everyone makes choices that have consequences. I don't shoulder all the blame for my mess but I also don't see myself as blameless. Even if I was only guilty of making poor choices in the men I chose it was still a choice on my part.

The first thing I had to do was forgive myself as well as my captors. I had to ask for forgiveness from God and accept forgiveness from God. Then I had to let it go. Then I had to not pick it up again. This part took a little while. I could let it go for longer and longer periods of time but whenever something happened that cost me dearly, I raged at the wasted time and lost resources.

Surprisingly, the peace I feel now snuck up on me. It was a culmination of time, love and forgiveness and it's a beautiful thing indeed. I have met some amazing people with awesome stories to tell, and I have a couple of awesome stories of my own and that's the way it should be. At first I said nothing and then I said too much and now I wait to speak and say only what's necessary unless I feel led to share more. That doesn't happen very often but when it does I pull up a chair and pay attention. Life is just so awesome! Go forth and slay dragons!

Have you made bad choices? Do you blame others for your unhappiness? Do you blame yourself for everything? Are you ready to stop keeping a ledger in life?

God, help me to let go of what needs to be gone, to hold onto what I need and to tell the difference between the two.

THIS IS NOT THE END OF THE END OR EVEN THE BEGINNING OF THE END. IT MAY BE THE END OF THE BEGINNING OR THE BEGINNING OF THE MIDDLE OR THE MIDDLE OF THE BEGI NNING!

We don't know what life has in store for us. There is a saying that the future is obscured by an angel of mercy and I like that thought. I don't want to know what tomorrow brings. We can study the past to avoid recreating our own personal hell over and over but most folks I know don't learn the first time either. Some people pick the same choices every single time, expecting different results and suffer greatly for it. I don't plan real far ahead either and it could be because of what happened to me or it could be that I trust myself and God to make the right decisions most of the time.

That doesn't mean that I live in debt and ignore the future. We all have a social responsibility to do our very best and not cause trouble for others unintentionally. It isn't even that I think being somewhat hedonistic is a bad thing. If it feels good, do it! Be aware though that if that's your yardstick for making choices it's going to be the same for you on the consequence side of life. I'm sure there is a happy medium between living for the moment and planning your whole life out.

There have been a couple of times where I thought I was all set up for at least the next decade and then life intervened and I got to start all over again. People like to say that when you fall down the important thing is what you do after you get back up but I think the way you fall has a lot to say about your eventual disposition when you do regain your footing.

There are a lot of tragedies that force us to realign our plans and rethink our future. Marriage, divorce, illness, death, addiction, financial ruin and many other unhappy situations cause us to reboot the program that is life. Faith and family are vital when we get the stuffing knocked out of us; it's a very vulnerable place to be and it's not that difficult to fall into despair. Family is your blood family as well as the people you trust the most.

When you are suffering and you're not sure who you can trust I recommend using an attorney, a therapist or someone in the clergy. There are also hotlines that are available all day and all night.

When I went into the pain clinic I was at a crossroads and was so overemotional I felt like I was going to cry all night and scream all day. I called a hotline and was on the phone for thirty-six hours before my friend (he's my friend now!) talked me into going into the hospital and trying to get off all the meds and alcohol I had been using. I was terrified of the future without the numbing effect of the drugs I had become so dependent on.

Don't feel like you have to shoulder you're burdens alone. It does not make you a weak person to ask for support. I look at it as a loving exchange because I know that if the person I choose to trust and lean on was the one having a bad time, I would want to be the person privileged to be called upon.

Are you trying to shoulder the burdens in your life alone? Do you have someone you trust to support you while you resolve the issue causing you distress? Are you that kind of person in return?

Lord, help me to recognize when I'm in over my head. Don't let me drown in my pride or fear and help me to choose the right individual to talk to.

NO REGRETS

I won't be destroyed
My heart will finally heal.
You will surely miss
The way I made you feel!
Your regret will consume you,
Like a fire burning bright.
I'm so tired of trying
I must give up this fight
I'm not sorry we met
But in retrospect
I should have got a pet.
Written by Maria Quan & Jean Elizabeth

PUSSYCAT, PUSSYCAT

Hey kitty, kitty,
Want to play a game?
If you're not up for fun
That would be a shame.
I see you getting fat,
Especially for a cat.
Still you're filled with questions
Mama, who dat?
(a small nod to the New Orleans Saints)

ISOLATION

When times are tough
And you feel all alone,
When everything is rough
Please pick up the phone.
I will be there waiting,
Every day & every night.
I'll hold you til the pain fades
And you can see the light

***

FAMILY TIES

There's just something about family

My throat gets dry and tight

My eyes get wet and bright

Try as I may, try as I might

No matter what happens

I don't want to fight.

Sometimes it's daylight

Sometimes it's night

No matter what the problem

Together we'll make it right.

I've never felt like this before

The joy, the hope & the love,

What am I going to do

With all the love I feel?

I won't compare it,

To the way it was before.

I am going to share it, because I know there's more!

WHAT ARE YOU GOOD AT? WHAT ARE YOUR GIFTS? WHAT HAVE YOU ALWAYS WANTED TO LEARN? WHEN YOU GROW UP, WHAT DO YOU WANT TO BE?

Everyone is gifted. We all have the opportunity to shine and succeed and to be the best person we can be. It may take some time to find your niche but I promise it's there. There are actually some very good tools to help you figure out what you will love to do and it will give you satisfaction and pride and a sense of peace within you.

It is never too late to figure out the perfect calling for you. I took a test for occupational and vocational assessment on the Internet that asked me a ton of questions about the things I enjoy and the things I don't. It had questions about my values and my beliefs as well as my eccentricities and faults, and when I was done it ran a program and I got the results. There was an explanation of what type of personality I have, what type of folks I am most compatible with, and what type of jobs I would excel at that would leave me feeling fulfilled and satisfied with my decisions.

I also took an IQ test and the MMPI that gives in depth insight into the foibles of being me. While I was having so much fun I also took the ASVAB which is the armed services vocational aptitude battery test. I'm sure there are other options available to get as specific as possible and allow you to really get some insight about care you need. You are going to spend a third of your day at work, a third of it in bed and the other third eating, being social and getting your other needs met. With that in mind you should also consider investing in the perfect bed for you. I had a waterbed for years and it wasn't until I got a different bed that I discovered that my old bed was part of the reason I was an insomniac. Most people keep their beds for fifteen years so let yourself spend decent money on the best bed for you.

After the results were in on all the occupational/vocational tests I took, they gave me a list of the top three careers for me. It wasn't much of a surprise when I saw the words Author, Attorney, and Fireman! I'm guessing the fireman ended up on the list because in my misspent youth I was an adrenaline junkie. If it was dangerous, high in the air or fast, I wanted to drive it or jump out of it. I love medicine but the expense and the crazy hours would have done me in but in another lifetime, I would have loved it.

In order to be the most satisfied and content with your life please go after your dreams. Try as hard as you can, refuse to give up, and don't be too hard on yourself. If you are drawn to a vocation that is a conflict with your lifestyle or family, pray about it and try to approach it with the people that matter to you. It's possible that you may be surprised at support you didn't expect.

Are you unsure of what you want to be when you grow up? Are you working at a job you intensely dislike and would give anything to change it? Can you attend college or vocational school so that you can make your dreams come true? Have you ever really spent the time to figure out the perfect job for you?

You are a beautiful child of God made in his perfect image and you deserve to be happy all the days of your life!

YOU CAN BE ADDICTED TO PAIN MEDICINE EVEN WHEN YOU TAKE ONLY WHAT IS PRESCRIBED FOR YOU.

In my own life I struggled with this issue for a lot of years and it robbed me of a fair amount of joy and satisfaction. I fractured my back when I was eighteen years old and my doctor gave me pain medicine and muscle relaxants and I fell in love. It was awesome. I felt warm and euphoric and my dreams were fantastic. There was a lot of pain in the first year. In the 80's medical doctors didn't have the information they currently possess. Now we know that the sooner you rehabilitate and get up and moving the better.

I was fitted with a big white brace reinforced with steel and whale bone and it was painful and cumbersome and I had a problem with atrophy but as long as my doctor was still giving me pain meds I didn't complain. My personal opinion about pain medication is that it should be used for acute pain and should not be given for more than two weeks unless the injury is severe or the healing process is especially slow.

I realize that most of us like and trust our doctors and I am aware that doctors are much more cognizant about the potential for abuse and addiction than they were in the past. I am positive that my doctor did not intentionally allow me to become addicted to opiates. He was a very sweet and kind man and seeing me in pain was difficult for him.

Initially I was given Tylenol with codeine and either soma or valium for the muscle spasms that attacked me anytime I tried to lie down. I took that for a couple years, then my tolerance was too high and I needed stronger meds. By the time I was six years into the crazy ride of opiates I was still on relatively low doses of pain meds that were controlled substances and I had not graduated to triplicate prescriptions yet... but I could see it on the horizon.

Within the next six months I would begin to take the big slide straight to hell. I was taking my meds too early and too much and when I ran out I felt like I was going to lose control and run screaming into the streets. I began to see two doctors and get the same meds from both of them. I still ran out early and then I would shake, sweat, get horrible headaches, and I was very short tempered. I learned that I could go to the hospital and they would give me injections for the pain.

At this point in my life, I was dedicating a large portion of my time to the task of making sure I did not run out of drugs. I took the next step in my self-destruction when I started to forge my own prescriptions. I was horrified at the thought that I would get caught and everything would come to a grinding halt. I did not do this again after the fear caused me to have a panic attack at the pharmacy. I also never considered buying pills on the street. It isn't that I thought I was too good to take that step, I was afraid of getting something that would hurt me and I never got over the fear of being given poison or worse.

The next step in my path was hurting myself in order to get more pills. This was the line I swore I would not cross, and hitting my hand against a concrete wall in order to break a couple fingers was a new low point in my addiction. I learned that I didn't seem to have a problem as long as there was pain medicine in the bathroom cabinet but when there was nothing I still had to endure the withdrawal. I had cold sweats, nausea, no appetite, insomnia and I was a horrible person to be around. I joke with my friends that you can't tell I'm an addict while I'm under the influence but take all the drugs away and watch me become my evil twin.

So, I finally reached out for help and I went to a twelve-step meeting. I felt like I had come to a loving and supportive family and I attended 180 meetings in the first ninety days of my recovery. I learned the steps and got a sponsor and things began to get better. Never again would I have two doctors instead of one and urgent care and hospitals were places I only went to if I had an honest injury or got in a car accident.

The problem with being addicted to pills was, for me, a head game I would still get involved in over the next decade but the rampant insanity was a thing of the past. I started a new phase in my addiction. I had some genuine pain and injuries that I struggled with but I still had the program and a support system of people that did not believe my lies and rationalizations and that, in turn kept me mostly honest. I truly struggled with trying to control the pain that was a constant shadow in my life. I now know that there are three pain relievers that actually work to relieve pain as opposed to drugging the brain into masking pain and feeling the euphoria. The real pain relievers are aspirin, acetaminophen and ibuprofen.

The last rationalization I had to get honest about was the lie that if my doctor prescribed it, then I obviously need to take it. The solution for this was surprisingly easy. If I was scheduled for surgery or broke some bones, I informed the doctor that I was an addict in recovery. I took my sponsor to the doctor's office and if I was given opiates, she held them and gave them to me when I was scheduled to take them. This was something I was both grateful for and ashamed of at the same time but it worked and it was critically important to me.

Do you take drugs and lie to yourself about it? Has taking pills cost you a job or a marriage or your self-worth? Are you ready to be honest and seek the help that will change your life for the better?

Father God, please help me to be the best me I can and show me your love for me so that I can love myself. Protect my relationships and help me to be honest and loving with the people in my life.

I WOULD RATHER BE CASH POOR AND WEALTHY WITH THE JOYS OF MY LIFE AND THE PEOPLE I AM BLESSED TO SHARE IT WITH, AND I WOULD CHOOSE IT EVERY SINGLE DAY.

In a perfect world I would have it all but this is not a perfect world. When I had a beautiful house and more money than I could spend I was miserable and fearful most of the time. The people around me and the environment I existed in put me in such a bad place that the depression was crippling and I despaired of surviving it. I worked very hard to amass my wealth and I did not want to leave that life behind without a portion of my wealth with me. I let that desire keep me anchored to a bad situation that in the end deteriorated so fast that I eventually was grateful to exit alive.

It was a really bad idea to try exit that chapter in my life with some of my money intact. Truthfully, I knew better than to attempt taking my assets with me because my husband was not shy about telling me what would happen to me if I tried to leave at all. Initially I thought he loved me so much that he was driven to make possessive statements about me, my body, or my stuff. I would discover the error of my ways as time marched on.

In the early days of our time together he didn't want me out of his sight and I stupidly thought that this was also a loving and romantic gesture. I got so used to these kinds of statements that I no longer paid attention to them and disregarded the warning signs that all was not well in paradise.

Well-adjusted and normal folks don't threaten to kill you if you decide to leave the relationship. It was such a shermanesque statement that disregarding the threat implicit in the words was something I did as a matter of course because I heard stuff like this all the time. I come from the mindset that cautions against making threats and promotes action. Lots of people posture and pretend to be a badass and nothing ever comes from all that blustering. I always thought it was the quiet ones you should watch out for. Lucky for me that during the long years I was in this relationship I would meet plenty of people in both categories.

Eventually I developed a realistic assessment of who was really dangerous and who talked a lot of crap. I never talked to anyone about the fact that I needed to get out of the relationship because the unsolicited threats were declared on a regular basis with a great deal of excitement and determination. There were no threats about trying to leave with my assets because I think they figured I was too scared to leave at all and there was certainly a lot of truth to that mindset. I hope that by speaking out about living with constant threats that maybe one person will decide that getting out alive is much better than getting buried with all your "stuff".

Do you know that you are in an untenable situation and that the longer you stay the worse it gets? Are you cognizant that your options are simply to stay and be miserable and afraid 24/7 or to leave ALIVE? Can you make the decision to begin planning your exit quietly and carefully?

God, please protect me from those that wish me harm, and give me the tools to take care of myself and the wisdom to know who to trust because I realize I am putting my life in your hands and the hands of the person I am trusting to support me in this decision.

THERE IS NO SUCH THING AS AN EX-MARINE; IF YOU DOUBT ME, FIND SOME OF THESE FINE FOLKS AND ASK THEM!

I descend from a long line of patriots and more specifically a long line of Marines. My grandfather was one of Carlson's Raiders in World War II and I loved and admired him. I signed up in my last year of high school after taking the ASVAB when the recruiters came to speak to us and I thought the marine corps had the most awesome uniforms. My best friend in the world was in the Marine Corps in Vietnam and he believes that being a Marine was the best decision he ever made and I see the truth of that all the time as we meander through life. The Corps also have a widely spread and well-deserved reputation for being simply a cut above the rest. However, I truly believe that anyone willing to put their life on the line so that I can continue to live free, is a hero to me.

My grandson joined the Army a couple of years ago and he is thriving in the service. He has pride, discipline and a fierce desire to protect all of us from our enemies, both foreign and domestic. I don't think I could be more thrilled and proud of him. He would like to be selected for the special forces and I support all of his dreams and goals. If you compare James before the Army and the James he is now it's patently obvious that he made the right decision.

I think if we had everyone serve for two years right out of High School it would be a huge benefit to our young adults as well as a boon for us as a nation. Obviously this is just my opinion and I am not a specialist in such matters but I have seen the armed services make a huge positive effect on several members of my posse. I believe if I had actually served when I wanted to instead of fracturing my back one drunk night, many of my decisions from that point forward would have been hugely different.

I don't think it's possible to duplicate the experience you have as a soldier in any other way outside of joining the armed forces! You get fit, develop discipline, make lifelong friendships, and you experience being part of a large team with one focused goal! I have talked to scores of people and I honestly have not met even a handful of people that would say their time serving our country was a negative experience that bore no fruit.

One last thing I want to put out there is the decisions you can make about your life once you are discharged. You can get help with college or buying a home and veterans services are wide and quite varied. There are quite a few things open to our vets that enhance the quality of their lives and I think it's well deserved and as it should be.

Are you considering a tour in the Armed Forces of the United States? Do you feel as if you currently lack direction? Have you done any research or talked to a recruiter? Do you want to pay back the country that protects your rights and life?

AFFIRMATION: I will take some time to search my heart and mind about the possibility of entering a branch of the Armed Forces of America. If the idea resonates inside of me I will take the time to speak with a recruiter and develop am informed opinion regarding the decision.

A WEE BIT OF POETRY TO BROADEN YOUR HORIZONS!

COME HOME

Where did you hide?
Little child all alone.
Why did you bolt so far, far away?
Come in from the cold
Feel safe and be bold
My hand is here to hold
You are more precious than gold
When God created you he broke the mold
Travel back into the fold
I promise your heart & soul won't be sold
Come home little child, come home!

Dreams will come
Dreams will go.
Some hard to catch
Some you'll outgrow.
Some linger a while,
Searching for a sign.

Random Thoughts: A Spiritual Journey

> *Some slip by in a flash,*
> *Lost in an ocean of time.*
> *Some dreams are forever,*
> *Blossoming in our heart.*
> *Some lost, cut deeply*
> *And tear us apart,*
> *Dream, and have hope,*
> *Dream, and still know,*
> *Dreams will come,*
> *Dreams will go.*
> (Author: IG blueovals.)

FIGHT THE GOOD FIGHT!

> *On the bad days pain is a living beast*
> *Roaming inside of me in search of a place to dwell*
> *I'm not going to stay very long, it says*
> *But that's a lie I recognize*
> *It searches for a new home*
> *It would be my own little slice of hell*
> *I can't let it win*
> *It's already claimed so much*
> *If I have to I will crawl*

Random Thoughts: A Spiritual Journey

> *Out of the shadows lining the hall of pain*
> *I yearn to live in the light*
> *I want to win this fight.*

I GOT YOUR SIX!

> *When a friend trusts you,*
> *Opens up, shows his vulnerability,*
> *Rolls on his back to bare his belly,*
> *Your function is to have his back,*
> *Don't be searching for the best place*
> *To sink your blade.*

SHATTERED DREAMS

> *My dreams lay broken*
> *Like shattered bottle glass*
> *against the tenement steps*
> *I was left weeping*
> *With a blanket in one hand*
> *And a tattered teddy bear*
> *In the other,*
> *Oh God,*

Soothe my raggedy soul
Let me glimpse your vision ,
See your promise of
A promised rainbow
Across the land.

IT'S A NEW DAY

When the sun comes out
And the clouds beg to play
Gorgeous fields filled with flowers
It's a glorious day!
When the sun goes down
And the shadows grow long
Whet your whistle
Sing a happy song.
When the stars twinkle
With the moon as chaperone
There's plenty of life left
In this old bag of bones.

MEN-O-PAUSE

I am a forty-nine year old woman who has a lifetime of experiences on both sides of the track as well as both sides of the law. I have had dozens of jobs and learned all kinds of stuff but the only thing that I really want to do is write a book. I have written and published some poetry and edited a couple of novels but when it comes to putting my own words on paper my mind gets crushed with way too much information and I get bogged down in the bullshit in between the jewels of wisdom and I end up with seventy-six page one's for seventy-six stories and have zero page tens.

I am enduring menopause with as much grace as I possibly can and the infinite patience I used to have for other people and their foibles has diminished to such a degree that I don't really want to go outside and interact with all the idiots roaming around the landscape of my life. I have always had a measure of impatience with bullies of any shape or size but menopause has reduced my patience to zero. I confront people now that I would have ignored a year ago and I vent my frustration until I feel like doing the happy dance.

I am truly amazed at my poor body being forced to remain as a spectator while a bunch of symptoms lay waste to my calm serenity as I stumble along the menopause freeway of life. I paid a big chunk of change for the lab work that attempted to pinpoint my location within this process. My doctor's office called for a follow up appointment and I was excited at the thought of proactively managing my pit crew for the first time since this unfortunate race began.

I go to my appointment and when my doc walks in, I was bouncing on my toes in anticipation. He says hi and then he destroys my calm one more time.

"Your lab work confirms that your estrogen levels are quite low. Everyone is different but sometimes if you know when other women in your family started menopause and how long their symptoms lasted you can develop a timeline that you may find helpful. There are some options for you such as hormone replacement therapy."

I already made the decision that HRT was not something I wanted to do. I called around within my family to try to deduce how long I was going to remain in hormone limbo but the results were not to my liking. My grandma said she had symptoms for fifteen years and my mom and aunt had similar tales to tell so I went completely off the reservation into homeopathic remedies. I took black cohosh and within two weeks my hot flashes were gone and I was singing the Hallelujah Chorus joyfully. My doctor told me that I needed to get labs done fairly regularly because black cohosh is a bit tough on the liver. Truthfully, I didn't care. There was much I would endure to get rid of hot flashes and night sweats.

There is one other noteworthy postscript to this tale and it occurred when I was teasing my boyfriend about how fortunate he was to be a spectator in this race and he laughed and reminded me that of course he had to go thru it because I wasn't suffering in a vacuum. If I was miserable, I wanted everyone else to be miserable too.

Here's the things that worked the best for me: black cohosh, popsicles, ice packs and heating pads, opening the freezer door and putting my head inside, prayer, primal screaming (not much help but it did lessen the frustration) and drinking tons of water and eating four small meals a day because initially I gained a fair amount of weight.

Are you going nuts trying to remain sweet and cheerful when you really want to beat up everyone you see? Have hot flashes and night sweats destroyed your blissful nights rest? Have you noticed that you are not very pleasant to be around recently?

Father God, I know that you are aware of my struggle with menopause and I want to thank you for giving me the resources to find as much help as I can with the symptoms that cause me so much unhappiness. Thank you for the wonderful support I am receiving at this time. I know you don't want me to suffer and I will claim the victory in this battle. AMEN!!

IT'S TIME TO EAT HEALTHY AND GET SOME EXERCISE WITH PJ ROARKE, AUTHOR OF CORPS STRENGTH, A MARINE MASTER GUNNERY SERGENT'S PROGRAM FOR ELITE FITNESS!

I strongly recommend the book that Gunnery Sergent Roarke wrote. It is targeting military folks, first responders and anyone else that wants to get serious about eating and exercise in order to be always at optimal states of readiness for whatever and whenever you may encounter a challenge.

When you begin planning an exercise and eating routine the first thing to do get you're thinking in line with your goals. Some of this is odds and ends that you may not consider but if they are factored in at the beginning they can be the difference between a plan that works or a plan that fails. More than anything else it will help to get your head screwed on correctly.

I'm going to take away your excuses for why you can't exercise and eat healthy. It's one thousand times better if you deal with them before you begin your program. I realize you may have an excuse I haven't heard yet but I have to tell you I have heard quite a lot! In this section I will deal with the most common excuses.

I don't have time. I am just too busy!

This is probably the most common excuse I hear, and in most cases it's a bunch of bull. Time, that clock on the wall, is something we're all bound by. Got to get to work, pay the bills, pick up the kids, and get everyone fed. Why is it that some people seem to meander through life being on time for the whole show while others are constantly late, consistently having small crisis' and never have any free time?

I believe the chronically late are simply not honest with themselves, are unorganized, and/or are oblivious to the amount of mismanaged time in each day. Most folks who say they just don't have time are really saying "I don't want to get up early, stay awake later, miss my TV shows, or curtail my internet time so that I have the time to work out and fix healthy meals for myself."

You only need three to five hours a week of the right physical training to get and stay in great shape. Be honest with yourself and admit if you are so busy that you can't dedicate three to five hours a week to improve your health, appearance, attitude and outlook, I sincerely suggest you carve out some time to exercise because it will make you far more productive and balanced and healthy, of course.

Look at the situation as proper time management to insure productive and successful results with the added bonus of looking better & feeling better with the ability to feel fresh and relaxed so you can move on to the next crisis.

I'm just too tired to excersize!

Life can wear you out and I believe that you are tired after a full day of work followed by your commute home. Being tired from a long and stressful day is normal. However, being tired versus being too tired is comparing apples and oranges.

This was always my answer when everyone was going to the gym until I noticed that those same people coming back from the gym seemed energized and better able to focus productively after a short workout and healthy meal. Being overweight, out of shape and having a poor diet will just make things worse.

Combine all that with lifestyle choices that include smoking, drinking and the depression that occurs with poor health and you're just like a ticking time bomb ready to detonate. Actually, it's accurate to say that you are a weak bridge waiting to collapse. Being tired is bad but those poor decisions will lead to being sick, old and being prodded into an early grave. You deserve to love life and to treat yourself with concern and care. You can do better!

All you have to do is follow some simple guidance in regards to exercise and eating right and you will be dazed and amazed by what you can accomplish. As you get into better condition and your weight gets to where it should be, your energy level will dramatically increase. You will do more and feel LESS tired. I'm too tired to exercise as an excuse is a fallacy and you deserve so much better for yourself.

I don't have money to join a gym or buy expensive exercise equipment!

What price do you put on your health and wellness? I understand that a membership to a top notch gym can be pricey but there are many options in between that are affordable and don't require adding a gym onto your home or storing the latest and greatest home exercise appliances under your bed. Besides, the last two things with pulleys and big bands are already under the bed.

To get in great shape you don't have to join a big gym or spend a bunch on home equipment. Lots of gyms offer memberships inexpensively while you are checking out the suitability and availability of their free weights, machines and classes. Most towns have a community center.

If you are stuck at home you have tons of options; you just have to open your mind to see. I have used bags of rice, heavy cans of food; gallons of water or containers filled with sand will work as well. There are a lot of stretching exercises that are enhanced with the addition of more weight or a steeper incline/decline. The bottom line is simple. If you really want to look better and feel better there is a way to accomplish that goal using whatever is available to you.

PJ has some really points about this issue. The kettlebells in his workouts are not prohibitively expensive nor is a quality weighted vest. Take a look online and see if you can find these items used at auction or new and discounted. Be creative while you search.

I have health problems that prevent me from exercise!

Prior to implementing a new diet and exercise regimen, give your doctor a call to make sure it's ok for you to start doing the things that will cause you to feel AWESOME! Most of us have seen people that are in poor health or disabled do some amazing things so don't start this project with a negative mindset that expects you to fail. You can succeed and you deserve to be victorious!

I knew a man that was paralyzed in a motorcycle accident and he could not move anything from his upper chest to his feet but he was determined to stand at his wedding in six months. His fiancee' had never seen him unless he was in his wheelchair.

It would take the entire six months but when she walked down the aisle he was in a standing frame with tears running down his face. This event put the situation in perfect perspective. If a man with a severe spinal injury can use a standing frame to let his wife see the very muscular and very tall man that she was marrying, then most of us can adapt to a program with exercise and proper diet. I challenge you to devise and follow an exercise and diet program that will make you feel fantastic. Be honest with yourself and continue striving to thrive!

I can't get anyone to work out with me!!

You didn't start working out to be social and sometimes having a workout partner can be quite detrimental to the mission as a whole. Exercise by its definition is repetitive and focused and your routine should flow so you end up in that zone of peace and happiness. Working out with a partner usually causes one partner to adjust his/her routine to avoid long delays or even doing different exercises than you usually do on your own. I understand this sounds selfish and harsh but this is your workout time, not your social club. The goal here is the final result and not filling out your dance card.

In conclusion:

I could go on for days with one excuse after another that supports your desire to avoid exercise or eating well. The bottom line here is that if you really want to get in shape and get your weight to a happy place you will discover that not only will you have the time to exercise you will find that it's no longer acceptable to miss your workouts. Like everything else, progress starts with an adapted thought process!

Now that we have gone through all the possible excuses for why you can't get in shape and feel the best you have ever felt, let's get the party started.

Your first tendency will be to overdo it because you want to be in perfect shape yesterday. It took you a long time to get out of shape and to develop bad eating habits so it only makes sense that it's going to take a while to get back in fighting form.

While you are preparing for the grand adventure let's start out nice and slow. Stop drinking soda and start drinking water and drink a lot of water. If you need to taper your soda and coffee intake slowly, try to get used to drinking a glass of water after anything else you eat or drink. Our bodies are made up primarily of water and the percent of people who don't stay properly hydrated tips the scales at way past fifty percent. It won't be long before you notice you don't feel quite as tired by midafternoon like you used to. This is progress and you should be proud of yourself for taking the steps to be fit.

Another thing that will get you ready and used to the new program is to walk for twenty minutes after two of the meals you eat. First, you eat then wait twenty minutes and then walk for 20 minutes. I do this and I was amazed at how much better I felt just with the increase in water consumption and with a little walking.

The next change I made to my routine was to walk on the treadmill at a decent incline for forty minutes and I did three miles. I can't run but this pace is solid for me and I work up a good sweat and I can read while I'm on the treadmill. PJ is correct about exercise not being number one on my list of favorite things to do, but it quickly moved up the list after I noticed the difference in the way my clothes fit. I was starting to get some tone in my thighs and butt and speaking as an over forty five year old woman, it was amazeballs!

For me the next thing I did was twenty minutes of yoga twice a day. Since I try to eat four small meals a day, I was now exercising for twenty minutes after each meal. I alternated walking and yoga and within six weeks I lost ten pounds and more importantly I lost two pant sizes. My energy level was thru the roof fantastic and I was starting to strut around my apartment because I was happy with the progress I was making and it felt good to be in charge of my own body.

When I got to the six week mark I went directly to PJ's book for the info on calisthenics and light weight training. The next section is me poaching from PJ so that I can get you started seeing results because as the man says "results are what matter here and it's what we will focus on. With your head screwed on right let's move forward because to take even one misstep without the correct mindset is a step backwards.

The foundation for health and fitness can only be built on three solid blocks: Half a brain, the RIGHT exercises and good food.

Let's look at the brain first. You need the majority of your brain to focus on managing your life. You don't need to waste any more than necessary on fitness and eating right. You need to understand the basics, believe in them, and apply the required effort. Once you know what you're doing it will take minimal attention. Being in good shape is as addictive as any drug. The difference is that it takes some initial effort to get the fitness habit embedded, but once it's there, it's there. To embed fitness into your life they need to become part of your life, not your whole life, just a part of it.

You need to fit exercise and good eating habits into your life. It's ok to set high goals but make sure to inject common sense into the equation before you ask for more than you can give.

I'm convinced that three to five hours a week of physical training is all you need to stay in great shape, provided you eat like an adult. Again, I will state that you can maintain a high level of fitness with just three to five hours a week. I needed a program that would work with my schedule without requiring a bunch of specialized machinery.

The core of my training is SAT and it stands for stand-alone training and it should comprise half of the three of the five hours you spend working out weekly. If done correctly it takes one hour and not a minute more. It consists of:

One: Five minute warm-up

Two: Pre-fatigue: 30 minutes

Three: Mission: 20 minutes

Four: Cool Down

Your workout should be one hour of work and if you're not completely spent you need to ramp up the intensity and I will tell you how to do that.

Warm –up consists of light stretching and some light calisthenics to get the blood pumping and muscles working.

Pre fatigue for most of you is the work you have to do to get to where the real works starts and you can't arrive there already worn out and struggling. There are several different things you can do for this part and I recommend finding a couple of things that closely mimic what you are expected to do as a first responder.

Running, fast walking or hiking while wearing a weighted vest or backpack, regular pedal bike or stationary cycle, stairs or stair climber machine, versa climber machine, rowing machine and skipping rope.

While I think all of these pre-fatigue activities are good in their own way, I feel running, stair climbing and humping (with or without a weighted vest) are the best overall for building working fitness.

The mission phase is what you do when you are done with the pre-fatigue and should mimic what it's really like for you on the job. Power is your body's ability to move other objects. Simply put, it's the application of brute force. You need a balance of power and brute strength to really be physically fit.

Make no mistake though, our mission here is not body building. While you will definitely improve your appearance as you lose fat and condition your body, the purpose of this program is to develop a "go" body, not a "show" body.

The strength and power training part of the program is done with a combination of weights and calisthenics. When speaking of weights I'm referring to kettle bells or dumb bells. You can use barbells but I think a combination of kettle bells and dumbbells are better overall.

Hello, it's Jean again. I have gone through PJ's book numerous times trying to give you a good place to start in order to get fit in a way that will matter and will enhance your life because of it. In his book PJ gives you examples of every kind of work-out he talks about. It is available on Kindle or amazon and I got mine straight from PJ using Instagram. He is a great teacher and tells the truth without a bunch of obfuscation.

If you are a first responder or active duty soldier I highly recommend MGYSGT Paul J. Roarke JR, USMC (Retired).

His book is easy to understand, thorough in its scope and a fantastic tool for your arsenal.

TITLE: A MARINE MASTER GUNNERY SERGEANT'S PROGRAM FOR ELITE FITNESS!!

PJ can be reached by e-mail or on Instagram and Twitter. IG: corpsstrength

I WAS READING A MAGAZINE THE OTHER DAY AND SAW THAT A COUPLE GOT MARRIED AND THEIR WEDDING COST OVER TEN MILLION DOLLARS!

This isn't a rant about any specific person or group. I understand that people earn money and have a right to spend that money in any manner they see fit as long as they don't break the law or fund terrorism However, is there a point where this kind of spending seems to be about conspicuous consumption or good old hedonism?

Whatever happened to the concept Noblesse Oblique? Where is the line in the sand whereupon you realize that with the country and the world in such a precarious position after a marked economic decline the appropriate action would most certainly be to spend less? A lot less and much less publicly would be a good place to start.

As an exercise I tried to imagine what I would purchase and consume if I had one million dollars to spend on my perfect wedding. I understand that it's a onetime thing and every little girl has planned her perfect wedding since she was eight years old but I wasn't like that because I was a pretty big tomboy. My beautiful sister was the girlie girl. Her wedding was beautiful but not lavishly overboard.

My first wedding was big. We had seven bridesmaids and seven ushers, two ring bearers and flower girls and about one hundred fifty people in the church. I bought all my bridesmaids dresses at The Rack (Nordstrom's outlet) and they were fifteen dollars each. I made the gifts for everyone in the bridal party. My father took the pictures and did a fantastic job. The flowers were two hundred dollars, the food was buffet style, and the caterer was one of my mom's best friends. We had the reception in the back yard of my parents' house.

The wedding rings were two hundred dollars and we bought them from an ad in the paper. We went to Las Vegas for two days with our best friends on our honeymoon. The entire wedding cost us fifteen hundred and ten dollars in 1987. That included the rings, dresses, food, drink, church, flowers and pictures.

I believe this is an example of one extreme to another extreme. The only reason I made the comparison was to challenge whether or not it's a good idea to spend outrageous amounts of money on anything you can envision having for one event lasting one or two days. I think it's provocative to ask yourself "do I want the perfect wedding or do I want a nice wedding and a down payment for a house?"

I'm not male but I think men for the most part, want their woman to have a great wedding and they try to do everything possible to guarantee a blissful event but I know more than a couple of guys that would have been ecstatic if their woman suggested scaling everything down and banking the difference for that down payment. I have never had a honeymoon so truthfully I can't speak with any authority about this last part of the wedding package. I think it makes sense to get away and celebrate the beginning of married life somewhere that allows the stress of getting the wedding perfectly orchestrated to just fade away.

The huge and expensive wedding I reference as one end of the spectrum cost half a million dollars for the wedding dress alone. Who does that? It seems socially irresponsible and hedonistic one more time and there has to be an alternative that would look just as beautiful but not cost the money that could fund a small town for a year or two.

I have had a very good income at a couple times in the past but I have not been so wealthy that a price tag doesn't mean anything to me. The most expensive thing I bought myself in 1993 was a robe made out of brocade and lace with hand knitted accents at my neck, wrists and hem. Even the buttons were exotic and gorgeous. It cost three hundred fifty dollars and I loved it so much that even now twenty years later I can picture it vividly in my mind and wish that it was still in my possession.

Upon reviewing this entry I have to cop to the fact that I don't believe there was any negative desire or motive in the brides desire to have the most perfect wedding she could imagine. I do believe that even a small portion of the money spent could have been funneled to homeless shelters or to help get pets rescued, fed, and medically checked out.

Are you preparing for your wedding? Does it seem like too much or not enough? Would you consider paring down the extras in order to help others? Are you ready to join yourself to someone else for the rest of your life?

Father, speak to my heart and soul about the things that I need to focus on more carefully and let me hear your still, small voice as you speak to me. Thank you for making us all different in many ways and all the same in several areas as well.

THE COMPARISON OF MAN VS WOMAN IS NOT LIKE COMPARING APPLES AND ORANGES. IT IS MORE ACCURATE TO COMPARE A HAMMER AND A HARP.

Using the model of apples and oranges the differences are legion but they are indeed both fruits. Man and woman are both homo sapiens but after that initial classification they are more different than alike. Using the hammer and harp model we realize that both man and woman have names that start with the same letter H but again every comparison after the letter H showcases the many differences we celebrate.

Obviously one of the important distinctions is that women can bear children and men cannot, however they do have a role to play in the procreation process. Women are usually more emotion-based and men are more often logic and intellect-based and the two together provide much needed balance. I believe this is no cosmic accident.

Because we carry and bear children, we have a lot of empathy and are very protective with the relationships that are important as well as those pairings that create the beauty of balance. There is an argument in learned circles that the deep strength and protective instincts so visible in our men will serve us well as part of a family. A traditional woman is nurturing, empathic and happy to be a nester (someone who makes comfortable reinforced nests to congregate in and rest). I think women tend to enjoy the decorating as well as presenting food in an appealing manner.

When I was growing up things were very black and white. If you were born a girl you wore pastel colors with emphasis on pink and lots of dresses with ruffles. You played with dolls and did your nails and played dress up. I can see it in my mind like it was yesterday.

My brother was encouraged to play outdoors, climb trees and build models. It was interesting because I liked all the tomboy stuff but was thoughtfully discouraged to avoid drawing outside the lines of gender classification. My brother grew into football and then other sports as time went on.

I find myself wondering how much further traditional gender roles will meld together and we will have the metrosexual look and attitudes become even more separate. I think people should feel safe and able to be on the outside the person that looks at everything from inside, safely cocooned from danger, and loved and accepted as an individual.

Are you comfortable in the more traditional gender role as it applies to you or are you more comfortable doing things that you enjoy regardless of gender classification? Do you feel like one of the guys or gals or are you more comfortable with a combination of both roles? Do you feel pressured to act in appropriate ways?

Lord, thank you for all the gifts you have graced me with and I know that there is only one ME and please help me to be the best person I can be and direct me toward the things that you know I will excel at. Help me to appreciate the uniqueness in all of your children.

MAKE SURE YOU ALWAYS HAVE CLEAN UNDERWEAR ON IN CASE YOU GET IN AN ACCIDENT!

This is one of the things my grandma used to say as I was running out of the house on the way to their huge backyard where all of the grandkids like to play until we were too tired to move. My grandparents, aunts and uncles and of course my own parents dispensed this kind of knowledge and it appeared to be limitless in scope.

I have always felt that it was important to listen to my elders because they had already made it successfully past whatever stage of development I was mired in, and became adults and dispensers of sage wisdom. I deeply miss the opportunity to spend lazy weekends at the lake with family. We had a big extended family and until I hit my teens, we all lived in and around Grand Rapids (Michigan) and used just about any excuse to get together and have fun.

The lake wasn't big but it was in the family so we had our own dock and a deck built on top of fifty five gallon drums that we all swam to and jumped on to get sun. There was about fifty feet of sand on the bottom and it didn't get deep until about sixty-five feet. On the right of the dock was a weedy, overgrown area and we did most of our best fishing in that part of the lake. We caught everything from blue gill to bass and from catfish to snapping turtles.

My Aunt Carol taught me colors as a child but I didn't learn red, white, and green or blue; I learned Ruby, Sapphire, Emerald, and onyx. She also showed me how to pull grey hairs as soon as they could be found. She is a very creative and artistic woman and she encouraged my writing from a very young age. She helped shape the young woman I was growing into when she answered my frequent letters with letters of her own. It was such a beautiful gift and I didn't realize how special it was until the letters stopped. I pulled away from family as my decisions became less and less normal and moved into stupid and reckless.

I spent a couple of summers with my grandparents after we moved to California and it was magical. I was able to work on a friend of the family's farm picking produce and selling it at a roadside stand. I learned how to drive on a tractor and took out six feet of corn in the back forty. My first auction was amazing to me. I bought a goat for eight dollars and had no idea what I was going to do with it.

I'm really trying to find a way to tell you that we have so much to learn from our relatives as well as the plethora of knowledge to be gleaned from our peers. I listen much better than I used to and I like to think I have avoided some of the potholes in life just by paying attention. Most of us learn from our mistakes but truly I have saved myself hours of torment just by watching and listening to others. I have also learned what not to do by watching the messes made by my friends and family.

My mom taught my sister and me how to cook by making us responsible for one meal a week. We both enjoyed cooking so I found myself doing homework at the counter in the kitchen so I could learn how to cook the foods that were our favorites. My mom also spent one day a week cooking something she had never tried before and as you may expect some of these efforts sucked but most of them were ok and a chosen few were deemed awesome. It might not be the way to a man's 'heart but the majority of men appreciate a woman that can cook almost as much as they appreciate a woman that will eat. I had a friend that suggested the key to happiness for all the women that seem to exist on salad and diet soda was to eat a sandwich. Most of my masculine friends may appreciate the way a model looks on the runway but they don't necessarily want sharp planes and angles in bed with them.

Are you more worried about how you look on the outside or how you feel on the inside? Do you take the relationships with your family and close friends for granted? Do you listen closely when others talk or are you busy planning your next sentence?

Family is the one thing that you only have one opportunity to embrace or abandon. Please make the right decision for we all learn from the people we are closest to. Being a good example is a huge contribution to a relationship.

I ALWAYS WONDERED WHY IT'S SO EASY TO REMEMBER THE WORDS MOST COMMONLY USED AS DESIGNATORS FOR EACH LETTER OF THE ALPHABET, SO I LOOKED IT UP AND WILL LIST IT NOW. CONSIDER IT BROADENING YOUR HORIZONS.

A – ALPHA

B – BRAVO

C – CHARLIE

D- DELTA

E- ECHO

F- FOXTROT

G-GOLF

H- HOTEL

I-INDIA

J- JULIET

K- KILO

L- LIMA

M-MIKE

N-NOVEMBER

O- OSCAR

P- PAPA

Q- QUEBEC

R- ROMEO

S- SIERRA

T – TANGO

U- UNIFORM

V- VICTOR

W- WHISKEY

X- X-RAY

Y- YANKEE

Z-ZULU

YESTERDAY IS HISTORY, TOMORROW IS A MYSTERY, TODAY IS A GIFT FROM GOD AND THAT'S WHY WE CALL IT THE PRESENT!

It is difficult for me to stay involved in the here and now, especially when the places I go to are the best of what's available in my memory palace. There is also some fascination to playing "what if" within any time frame. For example, what if I had married Dennis? He used to be my babysitter and during one of my summers in Michigan we hooked up and had a great summer. He was in the army at the time and gave me a promise ring before he deployed and I went home to California. I was too young and immature to see what an awesome man he was and he had no patience with a girlfriend that wanted to see other guys while he was in Germany. I miss him.

What if I had never suffered the stroke, seizures and a TBI (traumatic brain injury)? There is a defining moment in my life when I realized that all I had learned and focused my attention on was going to turn out to be the biggest shattered dream in my life. I wanted to be a doctor and was willing to do whatever it took to achieve my goal. I signed up for the Marine Corps with the intention of serving six years and then getting some assistance as a veteran to pay my tuition to medical school. This dream defined most of what I felt was good about me. I was a good student but it was so much more than that.

Everything else in life seemed two-dimensional to me except medicine! Medicine was 3D, in living color, and all on a huge screen. Nothing about it was boring, not even the bedpan and sponge baths fazed me. I absorbed information like a sponge. My mom has been a clinical supervisor/therapist for half of my life and I am so proud of the dream she had and the willingness to do whatever it took to see it come to fruition. I had no interest in her chosen field but I was witness to the dedication she had and used in order to reach the finish line.

The big what-if question is understandably about my kidnapping and torture in Jean's House of Pain! Initially my reaction to the ordeal was to pretend it was a dream or that it happened to someone else but denial turned out to be a bad idea. I didn't talk about it but it showed in my behavior as well as in terrible nightmares. I was drinking whenever I felt overwhelmed and slept as long as possible. I was not a model employee, I discovered I no longer possessed the patience of Job and my tolerance for whiners was at zero.

After several years I realized I wasn't coping well and I spoke to a therapist. I was surprised to learn that there was a long list of people who knew I was there one day and gone the next. Why didn't anyone report me missing? Why didn't anyone hire a P.I. and get some answers? Why did this terrible thing happen to me?

I found a way to let go. I stopped drinking and acting stupid (for the most part) and I lost about ninety percent of the anger that fueled the fire of my rage. It took quite a while but I finally cried. Nineteen years after my abduction I cried and the last of the burning pain slipped away with my tears.

Today I strive to live in the moment as much as I can. I channeled my emotions to a healthy hobby. I teach teenage girls how to defend themselves against predators. The bulk of my class is about things we can do that help to avoid looking like a victim. Predators know what they want and probably as a survival tool they recognize the difference between a wolf and the sheep.

Living in the present is surprisingly satisfying. I have a fullness to my days that reminds me of the way I feel after the big meal on Thanksgiving. I certainly have moments when I leapfrog into the future or get mired in the past but they don't last too long and I feel so strong about living a good and fruitful life that I can stay in the now without expending a bunch of energy.

Are you stuck in the past or always searching for the future to such a degree that the present gets lost in the shuffle? Are you trying to bury something bad that happened? Are you afraid of what the future holds? Do you feel like maybe you should open up and speak to a professional about the things that seem to hold you hostage inside your own body and soul? Are you ready to move on from the tragic past?

Lord, please help me to sooth my pain and to free my soul from the bondage of living in the past or the future. Help me to find the right person or people to trust my secrets with and let my dreams be less oppressive and harmful to me. Place your angels around me to protect me and minister to me as I go through each day. Thank you for your loving kindness.

FRIENDSHIP IS BORN AS THE MOMENT WHEN ONE PERSON SAYS TO ANOTHER "WHAT? YOU TOO, I THOUGHT I WAS THE ONLY ONE!"

I know that friendship is one of the biggest gifts one person can give to another. I have not had a great number of true friends but the ones I do have are worth their weight in gold. I was a bit aloof following the initial years after my abduction. I had to lie about so much of my history that it felt like the entire relationship was built on a lie. I couldn't even follow up on the things I was passionate about because they were small centralized communities and my name and appearance may have changed but the inside of me was still the same.

I learned how to knit but knitting is kind of a solitary sport so I searched for something else. I eventually chose bowling because I was new to the sport and I grew to enjoy it quite a bit. My average was about 140 but my high game was 221 and I was quite pleased with that accomplishment. I was on a women's league first and that was a lot of fun. It was a church league and the women were all sweet and enjoying themselves. My aunt was the only relative I had within driving distance and we bowled together. It was well worth the investment to have quality time with her every week.

The only remaining hobbies I had left were reading and shooting. I read voraciously and many different genres. I shoot whatever I own at the time and if I want to check out something new, I rent it at the shooting range.

I have taught a couple of my friends how to shoot for home defense. The funny part of that is that if my student was used to games (RPG – Role Playing Games), they hold the gun as if it's a controller and they tend to move their hands to adjust aim instead of sight acquiring a target and shooting based on the picture in front of the gun sight. The first person I taught is a brother to my Goddaughter, he's not a hothead, and he doesn't have the Rambo complex rocking his world. He shot 60 rounds and he improved steadily as we went through the ammo. I had not shot a gun in 20 years and at the end of his lesson, I shot the last three bullets. All three shots were either in the head or the neck. I explained about muscle memory and repetitive motions and told him that if he was willing to devote a lot of time and even more money, he could improve to that level. He decided his skill level was sufficient and I agreed.

A really good place to meet and connect with people is in a yoga class. I chose yoga because it's a multifunctional thing to do that affects the body, the mind and the spirit. I have met some awesome people doing yoga. My sister is yoga to the core and she is happy, centered and full of love. Even if your desire is strictly for a good cardio workout yoga is still a good choice. There are a lot of different styles and flavors of yoga and my friend Jade will be contributing some information about yoga in this book. Wherever possible I have solicited help from my friends that are a wide cross of brilliant, funny, determined, and thoughtful.

The Internet is another place where folks can start out as strangers and move from there to acquaintances to friends and sometimes become family. It's also a place where you can be whoever you want to be. It gives one a choice about what they choose to share and who to share it with as well as the ability to omit things that may be painful or less than complimentary. There is a certain amount freedom to express what you choose because nobody is there to call you a liar. Just speaking as someone who doesn't like to share a rather huge section of life, I suppose I would feel liberated to be myself if all anyone saw was an avatar but that same process would keep me wondering what I wasn't being told. Many years ago when chatting was still fairly new, I had some bad experiences one after another. It seemed like the only thing people wanted to talk about was sex and their personal view of what it should consist of. It kinda creeped me out and I never really got over the ick factor of someone wanting me to hurt and degrade them, all in the interest of fun. No thank you; I think I'll pass.

So to recap the topic of making and keeping friends: church is a good place to meet like-minded people, the gym is a good place to meet physical people, yoga is just plain good stuff but you can connect with people there too, the Internet is a good place to check things out, but I do urge you to be cautious and either playing a sport or watching a sport is another arena rich in people. Go forth and conquer!

DON'T CRY BECAUSE IT'S OVER, SMILE BECAUSE IT HAPPENED!

There are a great many moments throughout our lives that are fleeting and yet still they bring us great joy almost in spite of themselves. It takes a bit of effort to change one's viewpoint to reflect joy over small, never-to-happen-again moments instead of sorrow because it just didn't last long enough. Taking the time to figure this out now will ensure many more such moments in the future. The other big advantage is that this mindset almost forces us to live in the moment.

When I think of things that cause me to smile instead of cry I remember some crazy, fun times and some rock and country concerts where I yelled and cheered so long, I lost my voice for days. I went to see Bruce Springsteen and we had so much fun that we went the next day and scalped tickets so we could do it one more time.

On my birthday one year I went to a concert in Las Vegas out in the desert somewhere and the concert started at eleven am and lasted until past midnight. George Strait was the headliner but I also saw Kenny Chesney, the Dixie Chicks and more, and the entire concert was perfect. It was a gift to me and I'm really grateful because at that point in life, I already had epilepsy and loud noise and the light shows would have convinced me that I should just stay home. I didn't have a seizure but I did have a headache for two days and I gladly paid that price for a day of country magic.

The next example is one of those that caused so much sadness and grief that it was exhausting but the alternative wasn't a solution and we discarded it immediately. My brother's wife had most of her family in Las Vegas and pretty much all of us were scattered around the states.

Cheri is a delightful person and all of our family got to know her family when they all lived in Vegas and her brother Joey worked on the strip with a host of big cats, and I mean huge, huge cats. He worked with the wild cats with claws and huge mouths with strong jaws and a desire to take a bite out of everything. We always thought he would pay for that decision with his life. We were wrong. About the time Joey turned thirty we were told he had cancer. We drove out to visit him every other week and it was emotional and tiring but the things I wouldn't change, was vast. Everything I did or saw reminded me of him, but I promise you this, I would rather have him for one day knowing the pain that was coming, as opposed to never feeling the joy that he always brought with him.

Have you been devastated by pain and grief? Do you think it might be better to avoid the moments that bring great joy in order to go without the pain and sorrow that happens? Do you realize that you are in charge of the way you react to any given situation? Do you think you need to start letting those moments of joy fill you up without fearing the worst?

God, help me as I go forward intending to love the moments of happiness and joy instead of hiding from anything too emotional. I know that with your help, I can be the person I want to be. You tell us to love each other, to love ourselves, and to love you and I claim the victory in that statement and give you honor and praise.

BAD DECISIONS GIVE BIRTH TO BAD RESULTS AND THERE WILL BE CONSEQUENCES.

Unintended actions are still action. A wise man once stated that for every action there is an equal and opposite reaction. God does not desire us to hurt but he can't always shield us from the consequences of our actions. He can soften the blow, and miracles do happen, but as our Sovereign Father it's his duty to raise us correctly. Remember this part: The same set of rules apply when we do good things; His blessings are bountiful and abundant. He is a joyful giver and there is no parent more loving.

There are some people who think as long as they ask for forgiveness they should be granted a clean slate and welcomed back into the bosom of the family. My opinion is that I want to be a part of a huge, loving family that doesn't forgive bad choices and behavior as if they never occurred. That would create a family of hooligans determined to continue their shenanigans unchecked and with no accountability.

This family I strive to be a productive member of lovingly helps us to arrive at a place where we are no longer happy sowing seeds of discontent and discord. Of course none of us are perfect, and it is a daily commitment to God that we strive to love in a manner that people hopefully will accept. We do not try to tear you down in order to build you back up.

I absolutely believe in miracles. I was so sick that my primary care doctor told me I should get my affairs in order because I had about six months left to live. I made a couple of huge decisions that improved things dramatically and I was willing to try just about anything to survive. My decision was all about survival and a new feeling that seemed to be happy and high.

I was still suffering extreme memory loss and crippling headaches but I did begin to have times of happiness and I became interested in the things going on around me. I got two jobs and neither one was all that great but it filled my days and allowed me to live alone and that alone was worth the price of admission. My best friend John and I shared many meals and went on many walks while we got to know more about each other. I had talked to him every morning for almost a year but I knew he considered our age gap to be prohibitive so I took him to the doctor with me the next time I had an appointment.

The doctor listened to his concerns and then she straightened out his thinking. She told him I was not an average thirty-five year old. I didn't go clubbing or out drinking. The fact that I was working at all was shocking but encouraging. She ended by telling him that I wouldn't be the one nagging and wanting to go out; in fact he would probably be disappointed because I needed a fair amount of rest.

That conversation changed our friendship. We started being affectionate and he opened up about more of his life. We went out for drinks and I slowly got introduced to all the people that are his close friends.

I'm happy to report that I passed all the tests and we were now a "couple". It was what I wanted but never thought it would happen. I considered that maybe he was just being kind because I was so very sick but his friends set me straight quickly. They were all glad to see him happy and I learned that he wasn't as indifferent as I thought he was. I think he was a big part of my recovery. We went to bible study on Tuesdays and prayed together frequently.

It's been almost fourteen years and it's still magical. He is still the first one I talk to about anything on my mind, he is there for every bump in the road, and I pray I am that person for him.

Are you still paying for bad decisions? Have you prayed and asked God to intercede for you? Do you have close friends or family you can talk to when you feel overwhelmed? Are you thinking before you act?

Lord, help me to go through each day with your words in my heart. Let my decisions be good ones and help me gracefully exit the things that are not so good. Let me feel your constant presence because I know you are always there.

I KNOW HOW BLEAK THINGS CAN GET. LIFE FEELS LIKE A BARREN WASTELAND AND WE ARE CURSED TO WALK ALONE. I KNOW THAT THIS IS A LIE THE ENEMY TELLS US TO MAKE US CAPITULATE TO HIS DESIRES. YOU ARE STANDING IN A CORNER WITH YOUR HEAD TOUCHING THE WALL. THIS IS WHY YOU FEEL SO DESOLATE AND ALONE. TURN AROUND AND FACE THE ROOM AND YOU WILL SEE! WE DID NOT ABANDON YOU; WE HAVE BEEN WAITING FOR YOU TO REJOIN US!

Sadness, depression and loneliness can make us feel all alone in a crowded room. We think that no matter what we are living through nobody else could possibly understand. The difficult one for me is when I feel embarrassed or stupid for something I've done and am trying to quietly navigate through the consequences for my idiocy. I prefer to be humiliated quietly by myself but it just doesn't seem to work out that way. I create my own isolation and then I forget to reach out for a helping hand, thereby insuring myself of more suffering in isolation.

At some point I realize that I am the creating distance and I turn around to face the room full of my friends and family that truly are there to support me during the low times and I am there for them when they struggle. God is there for all of us all the time. One of the things that help me get outside of my thinking is helping others. I have worked on crisis hotlines, fed the homeless, and sent packages to our men and women serving overseas. All of those things give me a sense of perspective. When I am alone my issues and problems seem huge but after listening to someone else tell me their story I realize I am just fine.

Some of the other things that may seem unrelated I swear they are all connected to my sense of well-being in one way or another. I feel better if I limit my intake of sugar and caffeine. I feel better when I eat at least twice a day and keep those meals as healthy as I can. I have never felt worse after going for a thirty minute walk and I try to do it twice a day. The last thing that seems to help is sleeping at least six hours during the night. If I am doing most of these things most of the time, I am very even tempered and peaceful. You know yourself the best and you will figure out the things that ground you and take away that out of control feeling that drives all of us a bit nuts.

Do you feel out of control in your life? Are you experiencing a lot of sadness and depression? Do you have trouble getting up and doing something productive? Do you isolate from others as you feel yourself falling into negative emotions and actions?

God, I know that I have the mind of Christ and was created in your image and you don't make rejects or throwaways and I really need your help right now. I feel all alone at the bottom of a huge hill that represents all my failure and I need to reach out, without fear, knowing that there will be someone there to catch me. Thank you for the gifts of mercy and grace and for all the love I know you have for each one of us.

As the rain comes down in sheets they mingle with my unending tears. My Ravaged spirit wears a life vest in order to survive despite my fears. I cannot give up because I know, deep inside of me, that salvation is almost upon me.

See me!

She feels alone in a room full of others,

They are the happy, shiny people.

She stands out quite starkly

Against the background of drunken cheer.

She is full to overflowing with fear

It resides in the shadows of her life

Chipping away at the joy she has harvested

She cannot give up.

It would be a huge betrayal

She would give much to feel peace again

A good night's rest and a shared meal

She'd be almost giddy with the joy of it.

She cries in her sleep, frequently.

She only knows because she kept waking up

To the tear tracks on her cheeks

And the wetness on her pillowcases

STOCKHOLM SYNDROME IS A REALITY AND ALMOST SEEMS LIKE A FOREGONE CONCLUSION

The cold starts on the inside, the shivers commence, and it's downhill from there. Feels like my bones are rubbing against each other quite painfully. Solitude is either a blessed relief or so torturous I want to scream. I'm comfortable with myself and I enjoy reading and writing so I can be happy in a small room with no phone or TV and would be just fine for quite a while. Because of my adventure with kidnapping I learned just how long I could be alone and ignored. I had two books with me and I read them ten or twelve times each and then one of my guards brought me two more. He smuggled them to me and took the first two, then he switched them out for two more every week or so. That's one of the kindest things I experienced and I would have cried but my tears were on vacation so I just gave him a wobbly smile.

I never understood Stockholm's syndrome until my own experience where the people around me were in charge of everything. They dictated when or if I ate, when I slept, whether I slept, if I was hit or tied up, who was going to use my body and anything else I may have to do.

After the first week, the mind numbing terror subsided to a low level dread that was my constant companion. I discovered who was angry and mean and who was compassionate as long as nobody saw it.

There was nobody playing the role of good guy. The man that initially grabbed me off the street came and went but he was always kind. As time went on he saw me pray quite a bit and he brought me a Bible and didn't care who saw him give it to me. That told me a lot about the hierarchy in this operation. He exuded a gentle spirit that was backed up by a core of steel. I didn't know if any of my other captors had killed before but I knew he was no stranger to violence. There was a weight around his heart, not of remorse or regret, which seemed heartbroken to me. I would later hear his entire story and it moved me to tears.

About two weeks into my adventure I had to admit I actually liked and cared for two of the people on rotation as my guards. One was a woman with a fair amount of clout because nobody argued or disagreed with her and they all bent over backwards trying to curry favor with her. She was aware of all this and I began to hear her opinion of "the bunch of sycophants" that were chosen for this operation.

The other person I cared about was Tony. He was a gentle giant and I knew he had much pain and misery in his past; he was always polite and brought me little treats and the Bible I treasured. Right around two weeks into my captivity, we started to talk about the important things in life.

I shared about God and his unconditional love and the peace that surpasses all understanding. He talked to me of his childhood and what it was like growing up the Sicilian bastard of a high up Italian family. I was familiar with his family's history but as he shared more and more, I was fascinated and repulsed. He had such integrity and love for his family that it never even entered his mind that killing people was not a good thing. He was raised with the laws of Omerta and duty. He never hurt a woman or child and the only reason he picked me was that my husband told him that I was a snitch and I was trying to bring his entire posse down. Tony was conflicted about this because there wasn't a lot of evidence in either direction but he was determined to do the right thing. As time went on he got to know me and eventually he swore fealty to me and I had no idea at the time how huge that decision was for him.

After a month, I began to wonder what the end game was going to be. Nobody wore masks or did anything to hide who they were. They did their drugs in front of me and sometimes they drugged me for the entertainment factor. I wasn't being beat or molested anymore but there was still plenty of references to what they were eventually going to do to me before I died. The last time one of the guys expressed his fantasy of pain and degradation Tony got in his face and declared his position for the first time. He told him that he was never to speak to me or touch me again if he didn't want to have to breathe through a tube.

I was heartened to hear in words what my heart had already decided, but I was concerned about what his words would do to the team holding me. We found out quickly. The leader called for Tony and they went for a walk. When they got back Tony was allowed to take me for a walk. It was the first time I had been outside in over a month. We were in an industrial park and it seemed pretty desolate and I saw no recognizable landmarks. We were holding hands as we began to talk.

Apparently his family connections trumped my husband's family connections but the group responsible for the outcome overall weren't sure what to do. They continued treating him with respect but they were much more guarded and I was afraid that our days were numbered.

At this point one of my guards who had a good head on his shoulders gave me two hand grenades with the admonition that if it came down to me against them, I was to choose me and not waste a second feeling bad. He told me this whole situation had gone on longer than anyone expected and I did not have the information everyone was convinced I was hiding. He thought we were on borrowed time and let me know that when he left that night, he wouldn't be coming back. His entire attitude was one of disgust and sadness. I hoped he got away clean and started over. He had a formal education and could get a job easily. I feared that the problem would be the loss he would feel at leaving a club he'd spent a good number of years with where he was treated as a family member.

The closer we got to the end, the more restless I felt. I worried that they would take Tony out and I would never see him again. I worried that it would be a bloodbath that would plague me for the rest of my life and finally I worried that I was fast approaching the end of my life.

Are you in a situation that keeps getting more and more uncomfortable? Are you worried for your safety or the safety of your children? Do you have a safe place to go and an emergency plan if you should need it?

God, please guard my family and me while we strive to do your will and live happy and productive lives. Let me be aware if the time to leaves arrives and bless our efforts as we soldier on.

EVERY GIRL SHOULD HAVE A K-BAR, OR TWO!

When my goddaughter started staying with us a couple times a week I had a lot to learn. We thoroughly enjoyed our time with her but I had never spent a lot of time with kids of any age. She hears everything and she mimics the best parts in front of just about everyone. She was eleven at the time and we met most of her friends during the summer because we had a huge pool and plenty of snacks. John loves her almost as much as I do and he makes the time to go swim with us or to play Yahtzee or watch a movie.

One day a couple of months into this whole adventure, my best friend Patti called me and she was laughing when she told me what Sasha wanted as a graduation present. She said I want a K-bar because really, every girl should have one.

Patti thought it was hilarious and I thought we needed to teach Sasha how to defend herself with or without a knife. In the next couple of years I would overhear her quoting me at random times. Some of the quotes I didn't even think she heard. She explained that she is a multitasking kind of girl. She excelled in the defense classes and John showed her some basic blade work. I have a K-bar or two but I know one thing about knife fights that is almost a promise. Everyone gets cut. I don't like being cut and I speak from experience. It's the way it feels as the blade goes in, it gives me the heebie-jeebies. I also have been instructed on how to hold a knife and the best ways to strike but I never really got over the way I feel being cut. It's always possible that someone could take my knife away from me and proceed to use my own weapon against me.

I got Sasha her first blade when she was thirteen and I made sure it was ok with her parents. I also gave Patti one because she was writing a book that had some blade work in it and she said it helped to actually hold it and feel the weight of it and see how sharp it was. I don't advocate carrying a knife at all times but if you're going for a walk alone late at night I consider it an intelligent decision. I prefer to carry a gun but the legal ramifications of getting caught carrying a concealed gun are far more serious than being caught with a knife.

There are a few more quotes that sounded much different coming out of Sasha's mouth than they did coming out of mine and I became much more aware of what I shared with her in the room. One example is that I had a friend that was an addict and everything he did was centered on getting dope and then getting more. I used to call him a big waste of space. I wasn't even aware I was saying it in front of her but the first time I heard her say that about someone she knew I was mortified. As a Christian, I really had no right to judge him and it was really out of line to intimate that he'd be better off dead. Hearing it from her, it sounded so cold and indifferent.

Of course, this whole phenomenon works both ways. I have noticed that some of the kind and lovely things I say frequently have also made their way into her vocabulary. It was a much nicer feeling to hear the positive stuff regurgitated as opposed to the not so nice stuff. Like I said, it was quite a learning curve to adjust to having a teen live with us a couple times a week. It has been the biggest joy in my life and I will always love Patti and her family for sharing their daughter with me.

Are you in the position to be a big brother or sister that needs some direction or company? Have you been considering how to give back some of the blessings in your life? Is there someone in your family or circle of friends that is being neglected or overlooked?

God, make me an instrument of your peace. Let me touch those that need it and be company to those that are so lonely. Help me to reach them and tell them about you and your unending love and forgiveness.

WHEN ANYONE GETS SOMETHING FOR NOTHING, SOMEONE GETS NOTHING FOR SOMETHING.

I'm not exactly sure what this means but I think it's the fact that nothing for free is ever appreciated or taken care of in the same manner as the stuff you save for and buy and feel that pride of ownership. It's somewhat difficult at this point in time because kids feel so entitled to whatever it is they want and many parents don't want their kids to experience what they did if their family didn't have much. I think it's important to teach your kids about money, working to earn money, and saving and budgeting to make sure bills are paid and the money lasts until the next payday.

I got my first car when I was eighteen. My parents did not pay for it and I was already living somewhere else. I worked at a car dealership and I bought a 1972 Firebird and I loved it. My payments were $105 a month. I had that car for over seven years and I had it painted a gorgeous custom dark blue on black and I remember how proud I was every month when I made those payments. I washed it regularly and didn't treat it like a garbage bin. It retained its value largely due to the fact that I worked in car dealerships and they maintained my car quite inexpensively.

The same principle applies to relationships. If you give one hundred percent of yourself without receiving the same thing, you are being shortchanged. First of all, men and women feel differently about the whole subject of relationships. Women want to get married and have babies, it's a biological imperative. Men want to have lots of sex and fun but they don't want to settle down until they feel they are established and can care for a family, both physically, financially, and emotionally. When I was growing, up girls didn't have babies and then wait until the babies were old enough to be in the wedding. Getting pregnant before you finished high school was not a badge of honor, in fact it was almost the opposite.

My grandma used to tell me that all guys want one thing. They could be charming and thoughtful but if I gave them sex they would think I was too easy and once they were done having fun it would be over and they would move on to the next one. I have to say that I knew plenty of girls that used sex to snare the guy they wanted. One of my friends in high school was very popular and quite handsome. He was also very respectful with all of the females he encountered. I watched a dozen girls try a slew of tricks trying to get him. Nobody did. He was a strong Christian, wasn't interested in sex before marriage, and he had no intention of marrying a nonbeliever. He was very candid and I learned much walking in his wake while we were in school.

It's been a challenge trying to teach my goddaughter Sasha of the value of money. As I was growing up we got an allowance for completing chores and then we made extra money doing anything any of our neighbors needed that we could accomplish and then there was babysitting. When I got my first official job, I had to put half of my checks in the bank per my parent's edict. Sasha never had an established allowance or chores and she was used to being sweet and playing one of her parents to get what she so obviously could not go without.

I spoil her a lot but lately I have been more aware of how much I am spending and have dialed it way down because during the summer she will have chores here and will get an allowance. Economically times are still hard and the days of getting whatever you want have passed.

I have been given some extravagant gifts and as much as I appreciate presents, I also like working toward a goal and seeing every week how much closer I continue to get to buy the next thing on my list. I used to build furniture for different department stores and for customers that purchased stuff and had no idea how to put it together. I was often given very nice stuff for five dollars and then I would build it and resell it. It was a great opportunity for me and my friends got some cool stuff on the cheap. I think I've made my point here. If you get everything you want as soon as you want it, you don't get to experience the satisfaction of working toward a goal to purchase something you want or need. They have more value if your sweat helped to earn them.

Are you appreciative of all you get? Do you work towards achieving your goals? Are you giving more than you should because of love or are you trying to buy someone's love?

Everything I want is achievable, I just have to work hard, save well, and I will eventually be victorious!

IF YOU TELL THE TRUTH YOU DON'T HAVE TO REMEMBER ANYTHING!

I don't have to worry about this anymore because I took a hard hit to my head, had a stroke, had a seizure, and now have almost no memory. I don't like to lie anyway; it's a betrayal to someone else and it diminishes the person I am trying to be. They say one lie results in up to eighty lies to sustain the initial untruth. I think that's a bit dramatic but it's a good point. I have never been duplicitous enough to be a good liar and I know from experience that being lied to sucks.

My problem with being lied to extends to the times after the lie. If someone was caught lying to me I would be suspicious of any words they uttered after that. It's actually a deal breaker in the whole relationship arena. I used to lie a lot. I never really considered it at all. I hurt someone's feelings and lost the friendship and it stung so I made a concerted effort to be honest.

If I can't be honest about something, I choose to say nothing at all and if pressed about my silence I simply say "I dislike lying or being coy and so regarding this particular matter I choose to remain silent." There are some people that will still poke and push trying to get a reaction. I can't really be goaded anymore because I have seen the devastation that happens when the wrong words are spoken at the wrong time.

I have to admit that telling the truth got infinitely easier when I stopped doing and saying things that were inappropriate, false, and thoughtless. For a large number of years I saved up all the juicy, sexy and embarrassing things I had done and when I was around my parents I loudly told them all the bad stuff. I think it was probably because I blamed them for not keeping me safe and for not making the people that hurt me pay. We are passed all that stuff, we have a wonderful relationship, and they have opened their hearts and minds to Sasha and she is so grateful for the extended family.

There is a difference between being truthful, being candid or frank, and being just plain mean. There are many things we learn about that are the truth but they don't need to be shared. The truth can act just like a baseball bat wielded by a pro. In the book of Philippians, in chapter four, we are directed in the correct things to think and speak about. I make it simple and easy for myself and I strive to say only kind and loving things especially in front of anybody else. If I need to criticize or correct something, I do it quietly and without a bunch of people hanging onto the words. When it comes to what I call social lies, it becomes a bit gray for me. I don't like to make disparaging or negative remarks about people but when someone asks me if they look ok or if their clothes make them look unattractive, I usually try to deflect. Rather than admit something is unattractive, I may mention an outfit that is more appropriate or has better lines or colors.

Do you get tongue tied when asked your opinion in a public forum? Do you watch what you say knowing that you could be planting seeds at any time? What do you do when someone says something that hurts your feelings? Do you hold a grudge or wait for a chance for payback? What would Jesus do?

Lord, help me to be loving and kind without being duplicitous and put a guard over my mouth that I not sin against you. Thank you for all the blessings in my life as well as the people I am blessed to know and love.

WHEN AN APOLOGY IS NECESSARY, BE SURE TO GIVE IT WITH A TRUE HEART.

I know many people who cannot say they are sorry. They show their remorse and regret and often do something to show their love or appreciation but saying the words 'I'm sorry' seems to be impossible. My boyfriend is a bit like that. When he is overtired and feeling a bit pressured he occasionally vents by saying stuff that isn't nice. A couple hours will go by and he will suggest going out to eat or he offers to do something that's been on my list of things to do for a while. I appreciate this behavior. Anyone can say I'm sorry and expect instant forgiveness and then go on to commit the same act again.

While I was researching this topic, I came across a cute discussion on the issue. It said when you apologize to do so with a true heart, which required three things. You must be sincerely upset and remorseful, you must apologize in person and sincerely, you promise not to commit the offense again, and offer to make amends in whatever form the victim decides. I like the accountability in this as well as I like the idea of really making amends in a tangible form.

My goddaughter thinks the words 'I'm sorry' are an excuse for whatever thoughtless thing she was caught doing and once she utters them, it is all better. She does it the most about cleaning up after herself. She's like a mini tornado and she blows in, creates chaos, and blows out again with hugs and kisses and 'I love you' being shouted from one room to the next. She's a force of nature and her energy is effusive and overflowing everywhere. We are teaching her that 'I'm sorry' is sometimes just an excuse to do it again. I have asked her to stop apologizing and rather to stop the behavior. In this case it's leaving the house to go home and leaving a mess that looks like a tornado came through our home. My newest strategy is to take a big plastic bag and throw all the stuff that she leaves out in the bag and then put the bag in storage. We'll see how much determination I have and how much charm she brings to bear on the subject.

Many people think apologizing is a sign of weakness. I suppose in some cases it could be a way to avoid conflict at all costs and having known both men and women who are that dictatorial and controlling but in my advanced age I don't have the time or energy to spar with bullies. I'll pray for it and let it go so I don't get sucked into any drama.

Do you have a hard time apologizing? Do you apologize too much? Would you rather show your remorse or sadness rather than saying words that anyone can say?

God, please keep me with a humble heart. I know that we are all children made in your image and help me to continue practicing an attitude of gratitude with love and sensitivity towards others.

Random Thoughts: A Spiritual Journey

We are two peas in a pod
When we united the universe nodded
We built our foundation for the future with care
I joyfully proclaim we make quite a pair.
Time flies by so fast, and just so you know,
You and me babe, we're made to last.
Written by: j.eliz

My memory is a minor chord
on the piano that plays
the symphony of my life.
The orchestra is a bit unconventional
Perhaps even eccentric
I lose memories
In all their forms and disguises
From the tiny single frame moments
To feature film sized chunks
Somedays it's scary, sometimes it's hairy
But it's always me.
Written by: j.eliz

TEARS ARE WORDS TOO PAINFUL FOR A BROKEN HEART TO SPEAK.

***

COMMITMENT MEANS STAYING LOYAL TO WHAT YOU SAID YOU WERE GOING TO DO LONG AFTER THE MOOD YOU WERE IN WHEN YOU DECLARED IT, IS LONG GONE.

It's easy to make bold shermanesque statements when we are in the throes of passion. We want to conquer the world, save those we love from pain, and be a positive and strong force in the world around you. I want to cocoon those I love from the cruel world for just another day. Making a commitment is much different from making a statement. Statements can be meandering and contradictory and full of fluff or rancor but they stand alone. Without commitment and action that backs it all up in the grand scheme of things, it's just words.

I am much more careful with my words than I have been in the past. As loving and forgiving as we are capable of being, words still hold the power to wound and they cannot be unspoken. Hurtful things are usually partially the truth, and that's what wounds so deeply. We trust people with the essence of who we are and when one of our trusted friends twists things around and shouts in anger or resentment, it feels like being smacked with a 2 X 4 right between the eyes.

A good example of commitment is after seeing something on TV that draws out attention to something unfair or abusive in nature and we proclaim that we would never let that happen in our corner of the world. In fact, we want to help eradicate it before it touches our little plot of paradise. Ok, that's a great sentiment, but if there is no action following our words, it is nothing. In fact, it's less than nothing. It's not fair to draw attention to something that needs changing and then to stand around wringing your hands as if that is some sort of support or affirmative action.

I feel a great amount of sympathy and empathy for our veterans. They stepped up to serve and protect our great nation and there is so much we can do to make their time less odious and more comfortable. I used to have a job where I went into a bunch of different stores and I switched out the old magazines for the new ones. I had 12 stores and serviced them once a week. The magazines that were out of date were supposed to be ripped apart and thrown away. I spoke to my boss and the store managers in each of my stores and we all decided that giving the old magazines (old is subjective here, they were usually a week old) to our soldiers overseas, was a great idea. I found a local nonprofit organization and started dropping off the magazines once a week as I finished my stores. They were a big hit and I'm pleased and honored that I put action to my words about helping our veterans.

Do you have a tendency to make wide sweeping statements without doing something to see that conviction carried out? Do you often wish you could do more to help those that suffer? If it were more convenient would you do more to help? Can you take the extra steps needed to put action to words?

God, thank you for giving us such sympathetic and loving hearts and help us as we find our way to do more than just speak. Open our eyes that we may see where help needs to be applied, and lead us in the right direction to help others.

BOLD AND STUPID AREN'T THE SAME THING BUT SOMETIMES THEY'RE AWFULLY CLOSE.

I see it more in kids and young adults and I remember the outspoken exuberance I embraced when I was in college. I naively thought that because I was learning new things all the time, I assumed that the rest of the world was living in ignorance as well, and it became my solemn duty to bring the truth to the masses. The real truth is that people hear what they hear in their time and they can go years hearing the same thing until one day it slaps them on the nose and they actually HEAR it for the first time. I learn as much as I can and try not to turn away from the unpleasant truths that are revealed right along with the good and great things. I need balance in my life and try to see to it that if I get bogged down with something negative, I find something beautiful and pleasant to focus on for a bit to keep things more even.

I don't enjoy altercations, arguing, fighting and confrontation, but having said that, I don't like putting blinders on in order to avoid the newest unpleasantness. My faith and love for mankind won't allow me to walk past something that should be stopped pretending I see nothing. When I see a man raise his hands to a woman or child I get right up inside that and act like I'm bulletproof and on the side of the angels. I have been hit as well as knocked out for standing up for someone that couldn't stand up for herself. I call the police if I see something that could go wrong quickly and violently.

There is a saying that talks about all that is required for evil to succeed is for good men to do nothing. We can't allow the bullies and haters to have free reign to express their outrage and disgust. I have memories of watching abuse take place when I didn't have the skills or the wherewithal to do anything about it, and a little splinter of my soul is captured in that place. I don't want to add to the shame I feel at doing nothing. I am not a rampant crusader, I don't have a cape or cool costume, but I do attempt to stay aware and to help where I can, as well as to know when my idea of help wouldn't be the right thing to do at that particular time. There unfortunately are situations where by acting, I may cause someone to be in more danger and I have to really pray about that stuff because backing down isn't in my DNA.

Are you aware of abuse or mistreatment that is happening to someone you know and care about? Are you afraid for the safety of someone you know? Have you wanted to help but just didn't know what you could do? Is your heart troubled by something that just doesn't seem right?

God, help me to hear your still small voice and to know when and how to help these people I care for. Let me see your will in these difficult times and when I am doing the right thing, let me feel the peace which surpasses all understanding. AMEN

I TRY AND TRY BUT SOME DAYS SHOULD HAVE A DO-OVER FUNCTION!

I have a fair amount of injuries that act up occasionally and it feels like the pain just sucks all the energy right out of me. I can get a bit melancholy or just plain fall into a pit of despair. I call that depressed and do my best to listen to what my body needs in order to be happy and shiny again. Some of the time it's directly related to my sleep or lack of sleep. Food can cause problems if I don't eat well balanced stuff, and after so many years as an anorexic, I really have to focus on eating because it's easy for me to skip food for three or four days. This is not something I'm proud of. The last thing that tends to trigger my depression is staying in my apartment for too long without getting outside and taking a walk or visiting with my neighbors. I love the complex I live in and have been here for a while so there's always someone outside chatting.

I am finally getting some professional help to put the finishing touches on my recovery from the whole kidnapping adventure. It's been such a long time and I processed a lot of the issues as they came up. I still have occasional nightmares that I really don't enjoy but they are so rare now that I just try to roll with them. I am seeing a psychiatrist to help me determine how much of my physical aches and pains are psychological in origin. I have given this a lot of thought and I know I hold my pain inside so it isn't much of a stretch to understand that some of the chronic pain I deal with is a reaction to the trauma from the past. It just seems like a good idea to explore getting rid of as much pain and anguish as I possibly can. I have already had surgery to correct the easy stuff but my spine and my head are the cause of ninety-five percent of my pain and that's not exactly a quick outpatient sort of fix. I believe that God has healed some of the broken parts, both inside and outside.

I have found out that over time if I simply walk at least thirty minutes a day and do some stretching and yoga, that I can channel some of my pain and frustration right out of my body. There are a lot of normal stressors in most people's days and we can all use any form of stress relief that's legal and free or not so free.

The things I struggle with on the not so great days is that food, sleep, and exercise all help and when I feel badly, I am not interested in any of the three. The one other thing that I let get out of hand is that I forget to drink water and stay hydrated. When I used to get drunk in my misspent youth, I would drink and pass out and wake up feeling like something the cat dragged in. I learned as I matured a little to drink a huge glass, like 48oz huge, of water before I went to sleep and I didn't feel so awful the next day. Gatorade actually even works a little better because it replaces the electrolytes lost to alcohol consumption. Or, you can always choose to not drink too much and for some people any at all, is way too much. In this matter, I am an expert.

What do you do when your day starts out bad and just keeps getting worse? Do you get overwhelmed when too many things seem to go wrong one after the other? Do you take out your bad days on other people?

Lord, help me to remember that you never give us more than we can handle and that even the darkest days will end. Thank you for your grace and mercy.

The best thing I can say about crappy days is that they don't last forever. Be healthy, live well, show love and grace, and have a relationship with God.

COURAGE IS ACKNOWLEDGING FEAR WHILE THROWING CAUTION TO THE WIND.

Fearless people get hurt because there is no tempering of the desire to act, not enough thought to the future. There is a similar statement about heroes. What is the definition of a hero? Someone who gets other people killed. I happen to disagree with this little gem of wisdom because I have known some heroic people, truly heroic, not just impulsive. There's a world of difference between the two. Foolish and heroic also happens and the end in those situations, can be a bit dicey but I try to credit people with the right actions and instincts unless I'm the one left with my ass in the wind. Then I can get a bit testy.

When it was time to escape the land of kidnapping and torture, I had been waiting for something to happen all that day. People change when they know there is an end in sight in a situation where there are captives and most of the time some people don't make it through to the other side after the termination of the project. That's my polite way of saying that some people run, some don't, some get hurt, some don't, and some die and others don't. Sadly, this wasn't my first kidnapping and I remembered what it cost me to survive the first one; I knew that this was going to be worse. The first time it was two men with a gun and me, and truthfully if they hadn't been drinking, it would have been more difficult to escape. Lucky me! I will take victory where I find it.

I was drugged early in the day with a combination of speed and a hallucinogen. I was scared, nervous and seriously pissed off. Nobody wants to survive forty-five days of unpleasantness, just to be shot in the end. If I was going to die, I wanted it to happen before my body was broken, and I had been forced to do things I never even considered to have to endure. Tony had been tricked to go three hours away from me and they told me he was going to die too. There was a crazy woman chanting to Satan that creeped me out but couldn't touch my faith, and that made her angry. There was another woman there who had been questioning me for a couple of days and I liked her because she wasn't accusatory. She finally figured out why my death was supposed to happen before anyone who knew the truth could ask me what I saw. It ended up being all about money. Greed coupled with stupidity and backed with malice.

They had me clean out the warehouse I had been held in, and things were a bit tense when Tony walked in toward dinnertime. He was pissed and nobody was with him and he walked in, looked around and he got mad. It was very scary because he's not a blustery guy. When he gets mad, his face tightens up and he gets very precise with his language. He knew he had been set up, he was trying to decide who needed to be punished, and everyone there could see the rage on his face. I was quiet and still drugged so I just watched.

The woman that had been talking to me for the last couple days walked up to me, handed me fifty bucks, and said "I know what happened, I'll talk to Sonny, you need to get out of here or it's going to get really dicey and I think Tony's had a long day already." She pulled me into a quick hug and quietly murmured to me "this wasn't your fault. If you get away you won't have any problems from us."

I would cry with relief later but I was on a mission to get myself out of town and lost as quickly as possible. Actually, I wanted to cry but my tears had left me and I was brittle, angry, and very disillusioned.

I don't know if I was courageous but I do know I wanted to survive and I wanted a couple of people not to survive. Thank God I wasn't in charge of who lived and died.

Are you afraid? Does something feel wrong or off center in your life? Don't disregard your instincts or fears. Pray about it and talk to someone that knows you who can render a less emotional response.

God, bless my days, bless my nights, and let me feel your love and peace flow like a river through me.

IF YOU WANT TO GET GOOSEBUMPS...
READ ON!

There were four people sharing a nice dinner at the home of their friends. They had two children, a five year old and a newborn. After dinner everyone crept to the babies room and peeked in. They saw their five year old at the crib of the newborn. He quietly leaned towards his sister and gently touching her cheek he said, "please tell me about God, I've been here so long I've forgotten so much".

This is a story I heard right after it happened and it has never failed to give me Goosebumps. I believe with all my heart that there is a living God and he wants to save us, he wants us to discover the truth, and to love and praise him. With all the things I went through, my faith in God did not diminish. I knew I lived because God had plans for my life and I was more than willing to follow through with whatever he decided I would be good at. I don't credit or blame God for my bad decisions but I give him all the glory for surviving my bad decisions.

I wanted to be a doctor. I love medicine, the mind, and the spirit, but I have some organic brain damage and memory issues that put med school to rest by the time I was 27. I understood but I was heartbroken. God is so merciful that during the different jobs that I did, I had the opportunity to see and help with two heart attacks and a stroke. Maybe if I could have forgiven myself, my mind might have been restored, but then again, maybe not. I had my own stroke and became epileptic and even worse narcoleptic. So, med school was a definitive no... for now anyway.

God is amazing to me and I try not to get too involved in the dogma of organized religion. I believe that there is only one God, He knows exactly who He is, and He knows all of our hearts. I had to experience several religions to get to the place I am right now with my faith. Don't feel bad if you're not sure what you believe. Everything worth having is worth working for. As I was experiencing different religions in my search for a personal relationship with my creator, I felt the good things right inside of me. God's presence is something palpable to me.

God, show yourself to me and let me experience the joy of getting to know you as my Savior, Creator, Father and Refuge. Help me to not get confused by false doctrine and remind me that it's not my place to judge others. Remind me that we are all God's children made in his image.

TRY TO LAUGH OFTEN AND WELL. LAUGHTER HEALS AND CAUSES CHEMICAL CHANGES IN THE BODY THAT ARE GOOD FOR US.

I actually got to the point years ago where I could no longer laugh or cry and my ability to feel emotion at all seemed to be leaking away leaving me as a dried out husk of the vibrant and happy person I remembered. I'm not sure what happened but I think I got sober and living life without anything to buffer my pain (and the pain wasn't all physical) was such a huge shock to me. I felt like a raw nerve all the time. My solution was to detach and watch for a while and before I realized it, I had detached much too much.

I made a list of things that I thought were funny. I chose books, movies and going to a comedy club. It was so much fun. The laughter got rid of the never-ending tension in my neck and back. I was a bit self-conscious because I had not laughed in so long, it sounded foreign to me, but it was lovely and I thoroughly enjoyed myself and I recommend it highly if the laughter in your life has been misplaced. You might be so busy and so stressed that you haven't really noticed that the laughter in your life has gone on vacation.

One of the things that helped me a lot was learning not to take myself too seriously and laughing at myself when I goofed up instead of self-flagellation that just made things worse and solved nothing.

There are a lot of things available in our community that help us get back in touch with our inner child. There are movies, amusement parks, playgrounds where you can watch children playing and laughing, and going to the zoo or to a ball game. Most of these events aren't prohibitively expensive and we get the ENTERTAINMENT BOOK that gives lots and lots of discounts on all sorts of stuff; I believe it's important to have fun, but if you can't afford it you can find ways to do something. I'm not saying this correctly and it's relatively simple. Having fun should be a biological imperative. Happy people live longer too!

Here kitty, kitty

Want to play a game?

If you're not up for fun

It'd surely be a shame.

I see you getting fat

Especially for a cat

You are so curious

I hear you say "who dat?"

Fear is not my enemy,

Terror is the friend I send

When your reign of horror ends.

You are nothing to me

Except someome that dies

So that I can continue

To protect me and mine

From you

I see one, think two

And plan for an invasion

Some say trust, but verify

We verify, then….

Laissez Bon temps roullez

OBAMACARE OR BUST?

I was going to try to avoid the whole issue of Obamacare but the impact from this issue is huge and is only getting bigger. Keep in mind that I don't have wings at all, let alone far left or far right ones. I am just another citizen, just one of the masses, except I have some fairly serious medical issues. I had insurance at the time that Obamacare was first floated to us folks living outside of the White House. I was paying about as much or my insurance as an inexpensive car payment and needed to keep it. Having epilepsy and having already had a stroke, I am considered at risk for another serious medical issues. Right after the insurance companies started raising rates, my insurance went to over eight hundred dollars a month and I found myself out of insurance. This had some immediate and far-reaching effects. I had to pay cash for my prescriptions and they were over a thousand dollars a month. The only possible answer was to take less expensive meds even though that also meant less effective management of my issues.

I spoke to my primary care provider and he said the situation was similar to what happened to us locally here about six years ago. A large insurance provider got an influx of a hundred fifty thousand new patients and added one doctor and three nurses. The already hurried staff was buried in people. The company at this point also instituted a policy that all phone calls would be returned in eight hours. This had the added benefit of piling more pressure on already pressured people who work in this field because they love to help others. I have watched some of those awesome people going to work in construction because they know it will only get worse and there will be an inevitable time when the patient care will suffer and the doctor's will still be doing their best; that just won't be enough. It breaks my heart to watch the future unfolding.

The immediate problem seems fairly clear. Please keep in mind that I am not a politician or an expert in this field. It appears as if some of the intentions in the Affordable Care Act turn out not to be affordable and there are other erroneous elements riddled throughout the legislation. The two big ones for me are when the President said, "if you want to keep your doctor you can keep your doctor, and it will be more affordable for everyone with the exception of the one percenter's."

A majority of the people who signed up did not currently have insurance or a way to afford it if it were available. They are being heavily subsidized and that burden will indeed roll over to the taxpayers. I am frightened that if it is not stopped yesterday, it will become another huge chunk of entitlement crap that we will not be able to extricate ourselves from, any more than insects can escape a spider web.

I do not believe the President did this on purpose and blame certainly doesn't fall on his shoulders alone. He was voted into office twice by the people. We have nobody to blame but ourselves. He is very charming and quite charismatic and I can certainly understand the allure of having the image he so brilliantly portrayed as a man of HOPE and CHANGE.

We sure got change and I hope we can survive it. It's important that we keep him in our prayers. He did not have the necessary experience for such an immense job and I believe he cares quite deeply for America and her inhabitants. I suppose being a community organizer wasn't on par with running the country and I can see what the job has taken from him already. I just want us to clean up some of our more egregious errors and move on. The only way to avoid repeating the mistakes from the past is to learn from them and go forward. If we do not learn from the past, we are destined to repeat it.

This was quite uncomfortable for me to write and I doubt it will survive the editing but I am passionate about it without being expert enough to provide a solution and my ignorance shames me. We are such a bountiful country with unlimited potential but we must stop trying to gloss over problems like throwing a new paintjob on a derelict building.

God, Keep your angel's at President Obama's side and protect him and his family as he continues to strive to be the best leader of the this great country of ours. Help me to remember to keep him and everyone working to keep and protect our great nation from harm in my prayers. You charge us to obey the laws of the land and support its leadership. God Bless The USA.

HERE ARE SOME MORE NUGGETTS OF WISDOM FROM MY FRIENDS!

THE LIGHTHOUSE

What am I really searching for,
When the veil of uncertainty
Waltzes clumsily before me?
When one day I'm sure
And the next doubts plague me?
Which lighthouse will guide me
Home thru stormy turmoil
To grant me peace,
To gift me love's precious shelter,
To allow me once again to feel
The simple silken sand as it
Cascades gently between my toes's?
Which beacon of strength
Shall I crawl to
To save myself from drowning?
Written by: Maureen Alexandra

WHERE WERE YOU?

Where were you today, my sweetness?
When my desperate heart reached out,
Traveling in love's wistful arc
Aimed directly at you?
Where were you today as my need peeked in
Raptures cupboards & behind walls,
Under sob soaked rocks,
Beneath earth's flowing waters?
Where were you today, darlin', as my frantic soul
Pleaded and begged and sought to fall into yours,
Unyielding in its cherished embrace?
Where were you today when I fought to love you?
Only you; now, forever & especially always,
In all ways?
Where were you, my love,
As I shed tears all alone
In unwavering need of you?
Written by: Maureen Alexandra

***

Random Thoughts: A Spiritual Journey

All of these words couldn't save my life, even if I were drowning in them. Even if I were choking on a stanza, a ballad wouldn't keep me afloat. Midnight is blue and this dark ocean of words keeps me from reaching the land of depression, a land I swim desperately for. Swimming across this cursed ocean, a mother page struts about, followed by age with feathers so green. And grace such an emerald blue. This family of color leaves light glowing in their wake. Giving birth to a rainbow as the father of time walks ahead in their wake. Eyes flutter open and I realize it was a dream...or was it? I could have sworn I saw the word muse scurrying along after the others to hide beneath my eyelids, until sleep comes to visit again.

Written by: Noah_Arkenswagg

***

FORBIDDEN YEARNING

I yearn to hold you, to feel you everywhere,

My mind in silent communion with you,

Telling you all the things I can't say,

Showing you the depth of joy

We share together,

You are the sun

To my moon

& I am yours.

Written by J Eliz

SKY

The sunbeams were woven into her hair,
Nebulas stretched through her eyes,
She wore a girdle of constellations
And an emptiness in those black hole eyes.
Written by Muse of Seventeen

PRETENSIOUSNESS SQUARED

Large words do not define quality.

However, since you prefer the more exquisite selection of idioms,

I will fabricate tapestries

Consisting solely of gargantuan depictions

Of what would previously be considered to be

Provincial dialect in its stark simplicity.

In order for your pursuit of fabricated intelligence

may be satiated.

It appears to be anything but a falsehood

That you should care not for the contents of writing,

But solely how superfluously it may be constructed

In all the flamboyance and floweriness of language.

Should thou find my writing to be unsatisfactory?

211

Random Thoughts: A Spiritual Journey

For lack of flamboyant language, I shall simply ask of thee

To take a perfectly polished pump

Up thine own posterior.

Written by Muse of Seventeen

RISK IS A KEY COMPONENT

To learn how to risk yourself,

Open your heart, bare your soul,

Be supportive, holding nothing back

Neither in fear or shame,

Give, then give more, then give even more!

You can't out give God.

Shine your light in the hall of shadows,

Be the truth, go forth in love,

Swim across the moat & tear down those walls.

Written by J Eliz

LET'S TALK ABOUT

Anxiety is when you get stuck on your inhalation,

Depression is when you get stuck on your exhalation.

Breath is a powerful tool for mental balance, how is it affecting you?

Yoga has taught me that I constantly hold my breath as if I am bracing myself for something bad to happen at all times. Some say breath is symbolic of life. If this is believed then I am living shallowly and am not fully present and alive in each moment.

A simple breathing/meditation exercise for those such as breathing, and I, who have problems letting, go is to match your inhalations to your exhalations, for example: inhaling for a slow count of three and exhaling for a slow count of three. Over time, you can increase your numbers and lengths that will allow for your peace of mind to also deepen.

DID YOU REMEMBER TO PRAY THIS MORNING? GOD DIDN'T FORGET TO WAKE YOU UP!

In the last twenty years, I would say we have had crazy fast changes in the way we perceive time as well as ways people try to steer others towards seeing time. I promised that when I got older I would not trot out the analogies from my childhood in order to give a reality check to someone going through their childhood now. Today I must break that vow.

I can remember walking to school and home in the snow, and it was uphill BOTH ways! LOL. Truthfully, we did walk to school and it was about a half mile. We all made up a gang of kids that got bigger as we went through the neighborhood, and the older kids watched out for the younger ones, though they didn't get paid or rewarded. It was just the right thing to do. We had some slight bullying, but again, the majority of the kids in the school didn't think it was ok to humiliate or bully anyone and they didn't walk away or look the other way.

Our version of play dates was stepping out on our porch and yelling for kids to come out and play. We played a lot of ball games and some role-playing stuff without a computer in sight. When the streetlights came on, it was time to go inside. I lived in a decent neighborhood and we always seemed to have ten or fifteen kids hanging out in the afternoons and early evenings. Our parents didn't have to watch us play to make sure we didn't get hurt or kidnapped and the older neighborhood kids kept everyone in line. It was not unusual to see five or six kids from the same family all playing with the other kids and not feeling concerned that they were hanging out with their younger siblings. It seems to me that once they could drive, you might see some separation as kids become young adults.

We took our lunch to school for a while and there were no Lunchables! There was an option for low-income kids to get free lunch and nobody made fun of that option either. Perhaps there were two or three kinds of peanut butter and most folks put up their own preserves but for the ones that didn't, there were maybe four or five choices for flavors. There were two kinds of ketchup and two kinds of mustard and four kinds of salad dressing.

There was no Minute Rice or instant oatmeal and there certainly were no microwaves. Today it's possible to go to the store and buy all the stuff for your kids' lunches in boxes or bags that have individual serving sizes for most of your needs. We had those too; they were called plastic bags or wax paper wrapping.

The entire experience of owning and caring for a pet was a precursor for being responsible enough to live alone or with a roommate and eventually a spouse and progeny, although I understand it may present a problem if you put your spouse or progeny in a dog crate at night. When we walked our doggies most of us laughed at the thought of a leash and I promise nobody picked up their pets steaming fecal matter in order to dispose of something completely bio-degradable and gross to pick up and carry. If I was a dog, I would be laughing myself sick. I look at it like this: if poop stays on the ground or the grass more people would watch where they're going!

When I was a kid…. Things were much simpler…

WHAT ARE MYSPACE, FACEBOOK, TWITTER, INSTAGRAM, VINES, ASK, TUMBLR & OTHER KINDS OF SOCIAL MEDIA?

I just turned forty-nine so truthfully this question should make my face bunch up like I just bit into a lemon, but because I have a fifteen-year-old goddaughter, I know just enough to make a complete fool of myself in conversation. When I finally got a smartphone I had owned it about ten minutes before I felt like a moron. So much for being smart!

My goddaughter Sasha grabbed my phone, played with it for ten or fifteen minutes and handed it back to me with a smirk. It was transformed into a really cool combination of a photo album, phone, and financial planner. It was the first time I realized that the us-against-them mentality had shifted and I was no longer one of us. I had become one of them!

I wanted to be a big baby and cry like a girl but I had a reputation to uphold although I had to honestly admit all my former glory was slipping through my fingers like sand through an hourglass. There was a definite shift in power.

I am no expert regarding all things social media but because of my past and the people that I know as well as those I am still a little fearful about, I possess rudimentary knowledge of social mores and customs in relationship to smart technology. But, for the most part, it consisted of checking out new input and data and determining its damaging capabilities as well as if any of the new info fell under the attorney/patient privilege. The truth to the attorney/client relationship is OF COURSE its users started to plan for their case. It winds down to being all about money and I have a flash of brilliance that speaks in a disembodied voice "Son, no matter what people say and in many situations regardless of what they do, it is always and all ways about money!"

I realize I am more paranoid than the average consumer but I come by it naturally and would rather be overcautious than over dead. I know it sounds dramatic but sadly I have history that proves the statement "shit happens". I keep a loaded gun by my bed and it hasn't shot anyone... lately.

I always think about the kind of stuff on Vines and ASK and wonder if I'm still going to be as amused by it twenty years from now as I am at this moment. I don't like public embarrassment any more than I like public humiliation and I think the difference between the two is one of degrees.

Young adults are very much multitasked in nature. They use Twitter to talk back and forth and to avoid the complete immersion in social media that Facebook offers. ASK is in my opinion a problem because it's largely anonymous and whenever you offer something like that with no accountability, it gets out of hand and the questions degenerate into sex and drugs while the answers are inappropriate at best. My cub (the Sashkah, Sasha or my goddaughter are all acceptable aliases) stopped using it after a man took a long time and was quite graphic in his depiction of the rape and beating he had planned for her. It gave me the creeps and that's not easy to do with my past.

Facebook gets trolled for data mining and it wants to connect all your acquaintances, friends, and family, and puts a big red bow on the finished product. My parents and my sister spend some time on Facebook but not too much. I was the one that had absolutely nothing to do with any social media at all for almost twenty years. No TV, No newspaper, No radio, No Facebook, Twitter, Myspace, or anything else that is related to social media. I could not afford having my picture anywhere it could possibly be seen, and recognized or worse. I was never even in the background of pics that were going to be posted anywhere because I know how effective facial recognition can be used. I will certainly admit to erring on the side of caution.

It really was much simpler in the early eighties. If we were stupid or drunk, the worst we could look forward to was teasing from friends and berating from family that might have been there. Now, it's amazeballs and pictures and video can go viral in a matter of minutes and hours. I feel sorry for y'all underneath the microscope 24/7.

I have a good example of the difference between the past, the present and the future. When I was in high school I spent a fair amount of time partying. I went to lots of desert keggers, smoked a fair amount of pot, and took speed the week of finals in school. I drank on the weekends but not during the day unless it was in the morning. I let one boyfriend take sexy pictures and learned my lesson on that topic and it was a bargain at twice the price. God has protected me to the best of his ability and with me being foolish and stupid a lot. Let me put it to you simply. There are numerous examples of my drunken intellect available in my friends' memories. I am eternally grateful there is no audio or God forbid, video of those poor decision making skills.

Do you do things when you are drunk and high that you wouldn't normally do? Are you ashamed of your antics in the cold light of the next morning? Have you promised never to do that again? And again? And yet one more time?

Father, help me be joyful in following your word. I want to be Jesus to everyone I meet. Help me be love to all those I come in contact with and to lovingly tell the unpopular truth to those of truly searching for the answer.

I was writing this with imput from Tre' and some help from the cub and as it got bigger and a bit unwieldy we decided ending it soon was a good idea, but by the time we were at two endings. We were no longer "Part A" and "Part B" We had "Poem One" and "Poem Two". At that juncture, I figured I could use the end of one as a way to begin the second one. So here it is!

HE GAVE ME A DOZEN STARS PLUCKED

FROM HEAVEN

Kiss me and you will see stars,

Love me and I will gather them

Together in the sky

Show me the vulnerable purity

Of your righteous soul,

And I will bring the stars to earth for you!

A celestial bouquet,

Each one grants another wish

From the shattered dreams laying in pieces

At your feet

We will do a threeway

(Conference call with God, you perv!)

God wants to restore you,

He delights in you.

FROM STARS FROM ABOVE TO THE DUMPSTER DOWN HERE!

I will help restore you

Rebuild your heart

Improve your taste in men (present company excluded)

But never as your conscience,

That must remain unencumbered,

I gaze with fury into the abyss

With a thousand yard stare

And impotent rage

Hello darkness my old friend

I'm here to kick your ass again

This heart will never be yours,

It may not bend a knee for me,

But it won't even spare a look

At your pathetic sorry ass

It's almost not fair

Comparing you and I!

It's a battle of wits

And sadly, you are the unarmed opponent!

I'm already a stand up guy

Taking my best care of me and mine

Random Thoughts: A Spiritual Journey

Next to you I'm a star

You double bogey &

I two putt for par

You haven't

And come off the tee

Looking like the best thing

Since sliced bread

Written by Tre' Ross Aloisos

****

I HEARD A DEFINITION OF AN AQUAINTANCE I FOUND CLEVER: AN AQUAINTANCE IS A PERSON WE KNOW WELL ENOUGH TO BORROW FROM, BUT NOT WELL ENOUGH TO LEND TO.

I don't lend money to friends - ever. If a friend asks me for anything, I do a quick mental check to see if they are asking something that falls within the realm of normal. If it's normal, I do my best to help. I give the money to my friend because more friendships end over sex and money so I have done as much as possible to avoid friendship ending actions and I want to help because that's also the right thing to do as a friend. I realize my values and the code I live by are all good and they are deserving of awesome friends who share those same values and personality traits.

If you are truly my friend, I will do whatever I possibly can to help you when you ask as long as I am not endangering myself or other people I love. Money is not one of my triggers. I share and give easily and often if I can and occasionally I have caused myself unnecessary drama in my quest to be the perfect friend or relative. I understand that lots of folks consider money to be part of the Holy Grail but I have been wealthy and miserable as well as cash poor and so happy it should have been.

My personal list of the top ten things that make me happy would look something like this:

One...   My family is happy and healthy

Two...   I am happy and healthy

Three...   John and I continue to live the way we are right now

Four...   Sasha continues to stay with us a couple times a week

Five...   John and the ATS family continue to grow and thrive

Six...   My writing continues to be a blessing and I feel honored to share with the young adult demographic in meaningful ways

Seven...   My cats stay healthy and Squeakers continues to improve daily

Eight...   All the members of my family and close friends have a personal relationship with Jesus

Nine…   I continue to improve in my quest to eliminate all opiates and my pain is manageable

The concept of balance in friendship is an integral part of a healthy relationship. If the friendship is not in balance one person ends up a TAKER and the other one a GIVER, but it's almost like giving against your will. In the beginning of this kind of relationship, it feels good to be needed and depended upon but before long, it resembles the relationship where one person does all the heavy lifting and all the giving and none of the taking and anger and resentment begin to fester and get infected and it's all downhill from there. Nobody wants to feel forced to give to someone.

When I was a child, I was not a big fan of the chores I had to complete in order to receive my allowance. Sometimes I would get up early and quietly try to get everything done so I could "surprise" my mom with a job well done. Sometimes she would get up early and the first thing she would say would be a reminder of all the chores I had to complete. She would completely ruin my joy at the surprise and I would be resentful all over again.

Are your interpersonal relationships in good balance? Do you try to have an attitude of loving kindness as you go through the day? When you look at the cosmic ledger, are you giving more than you are taking?

Lord, I know you love a cheerful giver and I continue to practice loving kindness and generosity as I go through life showing people Christ who lives in my heart. Help me to recognize an opportunity to share your love and kindness with my fellow brothers and sisters.

Coming soon... More Random Thoughts

17245897R00131

Made in the USA
San Bernardino, CA
06 December 2014